T0171413

LIFE BEYOND THE CROSS

Akin Isaacs Lufadeju

AuthorHouse™ UK Ltd.
500 Avebury Boulevard
Central Milton Keynes, MK9 2BE
www.authorhouse.co.uk
Phone: 08001974150

First published by AuthorHouse   05/20/2011

ISBN: 978-1-4567-7787-6

DEDICATION

I dedicate this book to everyone who has aligned himself or herself as a co-laborer to build upon the investment made by Him who at the fullness of time sent forth His Son to restore us to His original purpose; and to those who would eventually believe the true gospel that Jesus Christ is Lord. Peace is to you.

ACKNOWLEDGEMENTS

Firstly, I thank the Holy Spirit who is the inspiration behind this book; He is the author and the finisher of the book. He literarily made me a channel to write this book. Have your way always.

I also thank my wonderful and loving wife, Lola and our children, Rotimi, Tunde, & Majesty who were there for me and saw me went through all the experiences of the season, good times and bad times. I will never forget. Thank you very much for understanding.

Special thanks to my parents. My father Chief Emmanuel Adeboye Lufadeju whose virtues and godly influences can never be forgotten, keep resting in the peace of God, and my mother Beatrice Adetomi Lufadeju whose encouraging words and wisdom always come handy in times of need; you have labored so much and you will not miss your reward. Thanks also to all my siblings for their love and concern.

I can never forget my home church for ten years, Faith Fellowship World Outreach Center, Sayreville, New Jersey, USA under the pastoral leadership of Pastor David T. Demola where the word of God is clearly and skillfully taught; and my teachers at the Advanced Christian Training School. Thank you all for your labor of love that God greatly rewards.

I also thank God for Pastor Robert & Ada Onuorah of the Redeemed Christian Church of God, City Of Redemption Parish, Ashford, Kent, United Kingdom for their time spent in editing this book and the support and Prayers.

I take immense pleasure to express my sincere and deep sense of gratitude to my cousin, Pastor Peter Oluseye Adeyemi, who knew about this book from the beginning and kept asking about the progress and encouraging me to publish it.

Lastly I offer my sincere gratitude to my friends Dr. Lowo Adebiyi whose token act of kindness is worth more than words can convey and Dr. Segun Olowe who is a source of constant motivation and encouragement.

FOREWARD

The bible talks about three main subjects, Divinity, Humanity and the Cooperation of both Divinity and Humanity in administering the creation investment of God.

In this book, the author has creatively woven through the bible and brought out in story form a clear perspective of God's thoughts and plans regarding His creation. It depicts the omniscient but hidden wisdom of God in rescuing creation from the captivity of Satan regarded as the Chief Hijacker. This wisdom which has enabled the fusion of divinity and humanity was God's fail-proof strategy for the restoration of administrative custody over creation to man. With the accomplished work of atonement, and the indwelling of the Holy Spirit in human vessels, absolute dominion is fully restored to man.

The author shows us how the Word in John 1:1 - 3 did not just serve to bring about creation but also was the powerful agent of redemption of captive creation.

There is an anointing that races through your being as you read through this book, this is because the full account of the gospel, God's power of salvation has been cleverly embedded in the storyline. Utilising contemporary and friendly vocabulary without compromising the message, the author has explicitly described the gospel. This piece of work will enable the reader to read the powerful and active word of the gospel in a light and recreational mood and yet receive the full blessings of the gospel.

Hopefully in future, it would be a good script for a movie that will proclaim the gospel in an entertainment friendly manner.

The life of the spirit is evident on the pages of this book and may you be blessed as you read.

Robert Onuorah
Pastor-In-Charge
City of Redemption Parish
RCCG, Ashford, UK

CONTENTS

Dedication   v
Acknowledgements   vi
Foreward   vii

1. Preface   xi
2. Introduction   xiii
1. Ultimate investment   1
2. Undercover operation   5
3. Exchange scenario: how did it happen?   10
4. Humanity needs a savior   15
5. The enemy is relentless   19
6. The source and destination   24
7. Preserved by righteousness   33
8. A snare for the fowler   38
9. The secret weapon of God   48
10. Mission accomplished   55
11. The cost of the power   64
12. Jesus' departure was expedient   68
13. Holy spirit – the limit breaker   73
14. Owning the responsibilities   80
15. The originator of all things   83
16. The eye of faith   89

About the author   93
About Life Beyond The Cross   95

PREFACE

Motivation, drive, excitement, passion, insights, enthusiasm are all feelings that are capable of engaging us in creative activities. But inspiration is different. It is a now thing. It is like an opportunity that grabs you and needs to be grabbed in return. It is a creative impartation. There are many types and sources of inspiration but inspiration from God is different because of its uniqueness and originality. It is possible for God to distill into one's heart an idea that has never been conceived by any human being in this world, as a result of availability, commitment and propinquity.

The greatest inspiration is from God; when one gets a revelation from the scripture, meditates on it, it expands, and becomes real on the inside. The truth can then be shared with other people. This is exactly the way this book was written.

The idea of this book came when I was seeking God's face concerning a certain issue in my life and I determined to fast and pray for a season. At that time, God clearly spoke to me that *"Because you have decided to seek my face, I will reveal to you kingdom truth that you would never have known if you had not made the decision to seek me."* Of course this is consistent with the scripture in Jeremiah 33:3 - *"Call unto me, and I will answer thee, and show you great and mighty things, which you do not know."*

As the fasting and prayer progressed, I was expecting God to talk to me and show me this exciting revelation he promised but nothing came first, second and third day. On the fourth day, I got something that seemed like it but I knew it was not because it came as drops; I was expecting it to pour like rain. On the seventh day, I woke up around 5.00 am in the morning, I had studied the word of God and prayed the previous night and the statement that dropped into my heart was "The secret weapon of God". I continued repeating and ruminating on this statement until it became real in me and I was aware that the statement was referring to Jesus being God's secret weapon. I knew one thing about secret weapons, and that is they are concealed from the enemy until they are used in the combat so that it catches the enemy unawares. So, I had an initial understanding that there was something about Jesus Christ that was concealed from the enemy, the devil. Then I started writing. I was referred to many scriptures and I wrote down everything that God laid on my heart. That day God told me things that my natural mind would never have imagined and I wrote them all down. The word was gushing out of my spirit like a well of water, and I remembered the words of Jesus that *out of our belly shall flow, rivers of living water.* When I finished that day, I checked the time and it was 5.30 pm. And that was the birth of this book. I knew at that time that this truth from God needed to be shared with the body of Christ.

Moreover, I did not send it in for publishing immediately but left this precious work and got busy with my job and other things, but God later got my attention and led me through the experience that finally made me to publish it. I know that God has a purpose for this book. He has assured me over and over again that this book would help his people to understand his precept and that it needs to be published. It is not meant to stay too long as a manuscript but belongs in the hands and hearts of men who are thirsty for the word of life. He said this light should not be hidden under the bushel but should be set on the mountaintop. Publish it!

INTRODUCTION

The lifetime of Jesus was centered on the cross meaning that his actual purpose would be achieved through his death. The cross was a critical requirement for the purpose of God for human beings to come to pass because it sets the pace for God's divine intervention for mankind. In other words, the cross is a place in history that God needed in order to fight on

> This is an explosion of righteousness which came as a result of God sowing Jesus as a seed; the seed died, resurrected, grew and multiplied into a multitude, each of them growing to be like the original seed that was sown.

humanity's behalf as recourse, since the destiny of humanity which has been taken captive by the enemy.

The life of Jesus did not end on the cross though the deceived conspirators wanted us to believe it did. The devil thought he had the victory when Jesus was suffering on the cross; he exposed Jesus to an open shame in the presence of maybe a couple of thousands of people and thought he had wrought a mighty victory. The situation was reversed in the spiritual realm, in hell actually, when Jesus, spoiled principalities and powers and paraded them openly; rendering them powerless and triumphing over them in it. Millions of people were there to witness this parade. People whose spirits have been held captive in Paradise since the time of Noah witnessed it; Father Abraham finally saw his promised seed in action; King David was there to hail the King of glory; even the thief on the right hand during crucifixion made his appointment with Jesus in Paradise and witnessed this scene. It was a completely spiritual event, a rendezvous planned by God himself. No physical being was aware of this event because it was **beyond the cross** but Jesus had insinuated it to his disciples, they did not clearly understand it. The revelation later came through Apostle Paul.

The spiritual realm is the real realm. Whatever happens in the spiritual realm carries a far more significant weight, and overrides the physical realm. The spiritual realm is richer than the physical realm because the physical was born from the spiritual. Therefore the victory that Jesus achieved in the spiritual realm, beyond the cross is more profound than what the people saw in the physical.

At the other side of the cross, **beyond the cross**, there is victory, and there is life. Just like a dry grain of corn would exist on its own if not planted on a fertile soil; but if planted on a good soil, it dies first, and then after some days, it gains life and grows into cubs, each containing hundreds of the original single corn that was initially planted. What an explosion. The devil was edgy before because he saw the key of blessing in Adam's possession. He was so envious and craftily took it away from him but now Jesus had obtained this same key for the entire saints of God that make up the church. The number is in the millions. This is an explosion of righteousness which came as a result of God sowing Jesus as a seed; the seed died, resurrected, grew and multiplied into a multitude, each of them growing to be like the original seed that was sown. Wherever Satan now turns to deceive, he hears the same word that he heard from Jesus, "IT IS WRITTEN".

In essence therefore, the cross represents the good soil on which Jesus was sown. The kingdom of God has come to us and the former things have passed away, and they have become new. Remember Jesus said **"behold, I will make all things new".** He did it. He finished the job. Life triumphed over death.

It is all about investments. Investments in the Spirit are wise and precise but investments in the flesh are a gamble because it is subject to compromise and negotiation. Seeds sown in the spirit are the highest quality of investment than gold and silver of the physical world. Even this world began with someone's decision to invest. It was a big project that was backed up with a commitment to invest, and overcome possible constraints. Investments generally involve sacrifices and risks; and this project was not an exemption as there was a major event that almost derailed its goal.

This book is all about the greatest investment ever made by the greatest business executive that ever stepped on the planet earth. Read on please ….

One

ULTIMATE INVESTMENT

Imagine you are the Chief Executive Director of a large company hypothetically called **Creation Investment Corporation**; you are strategic and proactive and in conjunction with the other directors, you have decided to set up another branch in an entirely different city. You employed competent managers whom you empowered to act on your behalf at the executive level. You gave them the power of attorney to sign

He never gives up on any project he started even in the face of negative outcomes. This project is very important to him as he called it his heartbeat. He would not let the company go because it is his utmost dream.

your cheques and authority over all your other resources and instructed them that as long as they operate within certain company policies, they will rule their markets because you are an expert in scope planning, activity definition and sequencing; you are proficient in cost estimating, risk management and integration. You are good. But as soon as you turned your back, the competitors approached those managers, cajoled them and persuaded them to operate on another policy that is entirely different from your organizational policies. Meanwhile the competitors knew the consequences of not complying

1

to your laid down company policies, but deliberately did it because they knew that instead of you ruling the market, they will be the ones ruling the market. To your amazement, the managers fell for the competitor's clever schemes, and within some months the company fell into a deep management and financial problems, and the competitors rushed in to take advantage of the situation. This resulted in a buyout. This is the purchase of controlling interest in your corporation by the competitor's corporation in order to take over all assets and/or operations.

Your managers were quickly replaced by their managers. The fall was so severe that your appointed managers became cleaners in the new setup. Imagine your enemy running your company, using your executive power and clout, writing your cheques out and making all the decisions that were supposed to be made by your managers without giving you any feedback whatsoever. What would you do if you were that entrepreneur? Why did they not seek for advice or contact me before they committed themselves to the competitors? The entrepreneur wondered. I trusted them and I gave them everything they needed to maintain the company successfully.

This Executive Director's vibrant visions for the new branch had now been compromised by the activities of the competitors or by the incompetence of the managers. The high standards that formed the basis of your business success can no more be met in this new branch because integrity had been compromised and the dignity of your managers have been taken away.

Moreover, a little background information about the competitors would be useful here. These competitors who used to be former employees of the Creation Investment Corporation believed that they were settling scores with their former boss who got them fired following series of misconducts on their parts. They now realize the value of what they used to have. They used to have everything at their disposal but now they have nothing. The mere fact that they were in good standing with the boss used to bring them joy; they were living in affluence, their boss trusted them. The Ace of the competitors was skilled in arts and entertainment and shined like the morning star. He thought he had mastered all the arts but did not know that the strength of the boss was in His character. He thought he could do exactly what the boss does, so, he betrayed his boss' trust by his proud behavior plotting against him; and that was the source of his problem which led to him being fired and thrown out. He was therefore given a restraining order not to be seen in the vicinity of that company; so he went to another city.

Those managers were ignorant of that information hence they fell for the competitor's clever schemes.

One of the major strategies of the competitors was distraction. They were basically enemies of progress. In the first instance, they were vindictive. They wanted to cause harm to their former boss and get his attention. Secondly, they were jealous of those managers as they saw them as their replacements. Their best strategy was to put a wedge between the managers and their former boss. Hence they resulted into this level of action.

The Chief Executive Director of Creation Investment Corporation has a high stake in this investment and would not give up on it. He is a realistic visionary, hardworking person who always embarks on different projects at different times. He never gives up on any project he started even in the face of negative outcomes. This project is very important to him as he called it his heartbeat. He would not let the company go because it is his utmost dream. Despite all the difficulties and costs being incurred by the parent company to redeem the smaller company, the entrepreneur was still bent on moving on, which tells us how important the project is.

He even tried to send business consultants to help redeem the company from the hands of those competitors but they instigated a plot against them reporting them to the police, got them arrested, imprisoned them, punished them and sent them back empty handed.

Meanwhile, all the attempts made by the Chief Executive Director to redeem this company failed until He decided that he would have to go by himself. But the tricky part is that he could not go in the office of the Chief Executive Director of the parent company so that the competitors would not recognize him as a representative of the parent company and treat him as a violator while he's still new in the city and has not yet found his foothold; therefore he must go undercover and underground. He had to go in the form of the victims but with reinforcement from the headquarters. He must hide his actual identity so that the competitors might not recognize him. He must humble himself, enter the city quietly, find a quite place to live, neither fight nor argue with any one, work as a cleaner just like the other displaced managers until he matures and begins to demonstrate the original authority delegated from the headquarters. Then he would later stand tall for who He really is and possess the territory of the enemy, taking back the company and what the managers had lost, restoring them all.

Two

UNDERCOVER OPERATION

This proactive visionary, resourceful, hardworking Chief Executive Director and Entrepreneur happened to be the Almighty God, originator and creator of all things. He is responsible for all the project initiation and planning processes.

> This tells me that God still has big plans for the human race that our natural mind cannot imagine....... The good news is that when the redemption of man is finally accomplished, and Satan is put in his place, God will resume the second item on his original agenda. Who knows how many items there are.

The office of the Director breaks down into three positions even-though, the office of the Director is one. God the Father being the Chief Executive Director that had all the initiatives would be sending another Director - God the Son who is the Director for Human Affairs, to take care of His top priority job on earth, while the other Director - God the Holy Spirit, being the Director for Special Duties, continues normal duties. The point is that they are all Directors just like there is only one God but three manifestations; this explains trinity.

The directors represent divinity while the managers represent the first representatives of humanity.

While in the new branch, this Director must disguise to be a cleaner just like those He originally empowered to be managers but were no more managers but cleaners; so that he would be able to stick properly to the original policies and procedures of the company in order to get the intended results for the company. So, this Director turned a cleaner came to this world in form of a man, born in a manger, the son of a carpenter in a remote part of the world, from where people think that nothing good would ever come out. The people said, Can anything good come out of Nazareth?

"Who, being in the form of God, thought it not robbery to be equal with God; but made himself of no reputation, and took upon him the form of a servant, and was made in the likeness of men; and being found in fashion as a man, he humbled himself, and became obedient unto death, even the death of the cross." (Philippians 2:6-8)

"For he shall grow as a tender plant, and as a root out of a dry ground: he had no form nor comeliness, and when we shall see him, there is no beauty that we should desire him." (Isaiah 58:2).

The Purpose of the Journey

This journey was initiated with only one reason in the Father's heart and that was His heartbeat, which is "The Redemption of Human race from Satan". His instruction to that Director turned cleaner was *"Take back all the executive powers from the competitors and restore those managers that have been incapacitated through the craftiness of the competitors; Restore their dignities and then instruct them to follow the company policies".* The company policy was to walk in the spirit. They needed to know about the power of the spirit man. This is the only way to be connected back to eternity.

God wanted to deal with this derailment from his planned agenda once and for all, so, he's sending one of the Directors of Creation Investment Corporation. The Executive Director could not find another person that is suitable for this mission but He knew Jesus Christ would not compromise the laid down policies and procedures, even-though, those competitors still tried to convince him to do so but on one of those occasions, he said ***"Get you behind me Satan! For it is written, you shall worship the Lord your God, and only Him you shall serve"***.

Moreover, this mission was a response to a call. The status of the call was high. The operation was meticulously and secretly planned, in actual fact it took God four thousand years to finish the plan and execute it. Many prophets were used to proclaim the plan, volumes of book were written about the plan, angels were sent to orchestrate the plan, and John the Baptist was sent to prepare the way for the plan.

The heartbeat of God was the redemption of man from the hands of the enemy of God who at that time was ruling the Earth with God's own power that was entrusted into the hands of Adam. Adam just like one of the managers had become like a slave to the competitors. As a slave, he was subject to the competitor's who were meant to be subject to his original delegated authority. Shamefully, the competitors had deceptively reversed roles. They would not even treat him right; his dignity has been taken away. He could no more walk tall as he used to. He no more had a face or a say in the affair of the company.

God was not happy with this state of man. The fellowship between man and God was broken. He tried to contact the managers but they were hiding because they were afraid and ashamed of themselves; they realized that they were naked and exposed because they have been tricked by the enemies and the management authority had shifted into the hands of the enemy. At this stage God knew exactly what to do. He knew that humanity must be redeemed from the nature of Satan, and from fear of Satan and dominion must be restored. This mission must be executed by him personally. He would come as the seed of the woman to bruise the head of the enemy and execute judgment on those who has disturbed the progress of His investments.

Since inception of creation God intended man to be an eternal being. That was why He created man in His own image, an eternal image that was connected to eternity. What Satan did was basically to disconnect man from eternity. What God would do in order to restore man to His original intended state would therefore involve connecting man back to eternity. God Himself is eternity.

The Father's Agenda

Jesus on the other hand had His role with God before the world began. He was one of the Directors of course. He was a member of the God-head (deity). It was the hopelessness of man under the oppression and authority of Satan that made God decide to send Jesus to this world in order to rescue man out of the bondage that Satan imposed on the human race through death. God could not look the other way or abandon (man) the project that he already started because of all he had invested. He had given man a portion of himself. He did this when he created man in His image. God was after His Spirit *(image)* that was given to man in the beginning and he would go to any length to make sure that human beings maximize the potential of the spirit image that was placed inside them.

God used prophets to proclaim the coming of the messiah, and it is this messiah that will eventually deliver mankind from the hands of the evil one.

It is then interesting to know that from this time on, all of God's efforts were directed towards redemption of man because the original plan had carelessly been destroyed by the frailty on Adam's part. God wanted man to reach his full potential. This tells us how important the human race is to God, for Him to have halted His other plans for the sake of bringing the human race up to speed and rectifying their mistakes. It is also interesting to know that the whole bible from Genesis to Revelation except for the first two chapters of Genesis, were written to show us all of God's effort to bring humanity back to his original plan.

This tells me that God still has big plans for the human race beyond the imagination of our natural minds. Creating man in His image and likeness, blessing them, and then forming Adam from the dust and putting him in the Garden of Eden were just the first few items on God's agenda for the human race. God intended to go to the next item on the agenda but the enemy came to cause **distraction,** derailing humanity from the plans of their creator, diverting them from their destiny. The good news is that when the redemption of man is finally accomplished, and Satan is put in his place, God will resume the second item on his original agenda. Who knows how many items there are. His agenda has no scope or time-limit and it would last eternally. It would be mind blowing because it is unimaginable. Then, the word of God that says *"Eyes have not seen, or ear heard, neither have entered into the heart of man, the things which God had prepared for them that love him"* came to mind. But the good thing is that *God has revealed these by His Spirit to them that know Him.* This is a desirable position. This is where I want to be. A place of knowledge of the mind of God; where He can reveal His plans to me.

It is also said that the sufferings of this present time are not worthy to be compared with the glory which shall be revealed in us, for the earnest expectation of the creature waits for the manifestation of the sons of God. The sons of God are they that allow the spirit of God to lead them. You are a spirit being. Your spirit man is yearning to know God in a deeper dimension. This only happens when you allow the spirit of God to dwell in you.

Three

EXCHANGE SCENARIO:
How did it happen?

Interestingly, only two people were given the mandate to act on behalf of the entire human race and their actions would be binding on all. These two people were Adam who according to our Creation Investment Corporation example was the first mandated manager but turned a cleaner and Jesus Christ, the Director who left his executive office and came to the world, and constrained

> The blessing of God to humanity and the power to hold the rein is now in the hands of the enemy. Satan finally got out of depression. He got a clue, a purpose for living, a direction in life and the direction was to kill, steal and destroy humanity; arraying himself against God, and became the enemy of the souls of humans.

himself to the circumstances of humanity. One failed, the entire human race failed. The other triumphed, the entire human race triumphed. Adam was made a living soul, while Jesus was made a quickening spirit. Both of them had a common enemy called Satan. Both of them were equally tested. Through the disobedience of Adam, many were made sinners, and through the obedience of Jesus were many made righteous. Adam became a channel for sin and death but Jesus swallowed and abolished death and became a fountain of life and grace, proclaiming life free for all.

"For by one man's disobedience many were made sinners, so by the obedience of one shall many be made righteous." – *Romans 5:19*

Coincidentally, Satan was the competitor that cajoled and deceived the managers of the new branch of Creation Investment Corporation. He used to be an employee in the company headquarters before iniquity was found in him and was expelled. The new branch was located in the same city where he now lives.

Since the time he was expelled from heaven, Satan, also called the devil, had been on the earth existing in darkness with no purpose and no future. He was in darkness and he had no way of creating light because the light he had by the time he was with God had become darkness with time due to lack of fellowship with God since he was kicked out of heaven, and darkness became his very nature, not only physically but also spiritual darkness which translated to ignorance and non-creativity.

The bible says "The earth was without form, and void; and darkness was upon the face of the deep". Satan was in darkness. He was stagnant, depressed and idle because he had no purpose. He was very bitter for being thrown out of heaven but also unrepentant.

All of a sudden he heard a thundering voice and saw a beam of light. He knew God must be around somewhere.

"His lightning enlightened the world: the earth saw, and trembled"(Psalm 97:4). That was after God said "Let there be light". When last did he see light? The last time he saw God. Unfortunately for him God separated this light from darkness, so he still remained in his darkness separated from God but could see God in the light. I can imagine that Satan was hiding somewhere snooping and peeping around at this time looking at what God was up to again.

This particular day, Satan saw amazing things he had never seen before. He saw God renovating the earth, speaking mysteries to the earth and the earth obeying Him; God created the firmament in the midst of the waters separating the waters from the waters; and God also created the land and seas. Then God started speaking to the firmament to bring out lights. He created two great lights and stars. The greater light, the Sun rules the day and the lesser light, the Moon rules the night. Then God continued speaking to the land and seas to bring forth creatures like grass, herbs, trees, cattle, beast, the fowl, birds of the air, creeping things of the earth. Eventually God spoke to Himself to bring forth man, and a masterpiece that looked exactly like Him emerged. This masterpiece was a spiritual being like God himself but later, God formed a physical body for him and called him Adam. From Adam's rib God made another human being called Eve. So, Satan saw these two special creatures, and noticed that of all things that God had created so far, He had something special going on with them. They were uniquely, wonderfully and fearfully made. The devil knew they were so special to God and that God desired to be with them because of his constant visits with them even at the cool of the day. He saw the glory and the peace of God around them. That reminded him of his position with God before he fell. He pondered if they were his replacements. To top it all, he heard God blessing them and giving them authority over all His creation, even including Satan himself. He envied them and became jealous. He knew how naïve they were. He was curious and wanted to find out what was so special about them. Then he developed a plan. He knew something that Adam and Eve did not know - **the consequences of sin**, and **the experience of being separated from God having previously experienced a close fellowship with Him**. And he thought that if he can just get them to offend God by disobeying His word, that will cause a separation between them and God; he can then take over all the power that God bestowed on them and they will be expelled from God's presence just like him. On their own, separated from God, they were powerless, and the devil knew that they cannot withstand him in wrestling for the power that God had entrusted with them. At this time, Adam and Eve were living according to the spirit, but the devil knew that disobeying God would bind up their spirit and make the body of flesh to take over. He approached them with a spirit of deceit, possessing the serpent. And the bible puts it that "the serpent was more subtle (crafty) than any beast of the field which the Lord God had made." Remember this was not an ordinary serpent but it was a devil-possessed serpent that had lying tongues. Eventually, he got Adam to disobey God and sold out the power that God gave to him. It was then easy for the devil to take over the power from Adam because *"Who you obey you shall serve"* – *Roman 6:16*. That was how the devil became the master of the man that was supposed to have dominion over all things, and the devil became the prince of this world. Actually, 2 Corinthian 4:4 refer to him as the god of this world. From that time on, the devil had little use for the serpent. Why? he preferred to possess human beings for his work than serpent because he thinks human beings are more subtle than serpent; most especially because of the **will power** they possess, he thinks he can manipulate them to suit his own purpose. The idea was "Why do I need a Volkswagen beetle car when I can now ride in a Bentley or a Rolls-Royce?". Human beings now became subject to Satan just like those managers became cleaners in their own companies and subject to the competitors; but remember it was supposed to be the other way round. This drastic transfer of power gave the devil the power to possess man and use man for his work, something he could not do before. This event led to Adam and Eve's spiritual death. Their spirit died and they lived from the soul. It was unfortunate that the plan of the devil prevailed over them. Death was not part of God's plan for mankind, so God did not have an agenda for it. Sin and death were literarily manufactured in the Garden of Eden. It was the devil that brought the tragedy of death to the human race because of hatred and jealousy for the creature of God. The destiny of man with God was life eternal but the devil brought both physical and spiritual death through sin. The event totally changed the course of their destiny as they now had a pronouncement of curse to deal with. Moreover, God used this occasion to make a statement that humanity will not remain in this state forever, but a seed of the woman would bruise the head of Satan.

The blessing of God to humanity and the power to hold the rein is now in the hands of the enemy. Satan finally got out of depression. He got a clue, a purpose for living, a direction in life and the direction was to kill, steal and destroy humanity, arraying himself against God, and became the enemy of the souls of humans. He thought he could do here on earth what God does in heaven. Out of jealousy he developed hatred towards God's creature and that became his vocation and calling until today.

God saw the new position of man and he realized that humanity had no future under the dominion of the evil one. This grieved God greatly because he could not relate to man as he had planned but he still desired to fellowship with man. How would He be able to do this? The cord between humanity and divinity had been broken. How is He going to connect humanity to eternity again?

Four

HUMANITY NEEDS A SAVIOR

The role was vacant for a very long time. No one was qualified or competent for the position but the Lamb of God.

According to our Creation Investment Corporation, example, professional business consultants have been sent to help redeem the smaller company from the smaller company from the competitors but were defeated by their clever schemes. The Chief Executive Director no more feels comfortable sending any other consultants but one of the Directors be assigned to go.

> He had the passion of man, he grew to be a teenager, he underwent growth into puberty, and soon he was ready for the work of the ministry. He went through these so that he might be a merciful and faithful high priest because he had to be touched by the feeling of our infirmities.

The person that was to be the Savior must have the kind of compassion and love that God has for mankind. Jesus in his earth walk manifested this kind of compassion and love, and the bible says he went about doing good, healing the sick, and setting the oppressed free. He had the same mind as God the Father. He did not do all these to prove his power; neither did he do it to prove his deity. He did them for the same reason that God sent him to the world, compassion and love which are the essence of his character. These qualities must be well emphasized in the curriculum vitae.

God the Father designed it that Jesus comes to this world as a man, so that his mission could be accomplished here on earth legally. He had the passion of man, he grew to be a teenager, he underwent growth into puberty, and soon he was ready for the work of the ministry. He went through these so that he might be a merciful and faithful high priest because he had to be touched by the feeling of our infirmities. He himself must suffer being tempted, so he will be able to help the difficult circumstances of those that are tempted. In other words he needed to undergo the experiences that will make him to relate to our circumstances and carry out his duty as the messiah and later as an intercessor at the right hand of God. He must humble himself and put himself in a position whereby he would be able to seek and save what was lost. That was his purpose in life.

Jesus grew in age and in wisdom. He was consistent in his positive confession about who he is and what he's all about. Confessions like "I am the way, the truth and the light, no one goes to the Father but by me", "I have come that they might have life and have it more abundantly", "I am the door: by me if any man enters in, he shall be saved, and shall go in and out, and find pasture. "I am the bread of life: he that cometh to me shall never hunger, and he that believeth on me shall never thirst. He knew where he was going and what he was talking about. He kept saying things that were new to man and all that heard him were amazed. The devil unsuccessfully tried to confuse him about his identity, telling him to perform miracles if he is the Son of God, but Jesus proved that He did not have to perform a miracle before he would know that he is the Son of God. He already is. We saw Jesus resisted the devil through the word of God three times in the account of temptation in the wilderness. He stayed on course and did not go against laid down policies. He was the Son of man; but he was led by the spirit of God, so, he was also Son of God. You and I are also sons of God only if we are led by the spirit of God.

Jesus was with God in creation because God said in Genesis 1:26 *"Let us make man in our image, after our likeness".* God the Father was referring to the other two members of the deity, Christ being "God the Son" and the Holy Spirit being "God the Holy Spirit". It was mentioned earlier, they were all the office of Director (of God) but in different manifestations, so these three are in the deity of God but their manifestations are in three ways. That is why they are a triune God. God the Father, God the Son and God the Holy Spirit. Also we read in the book of John 1:1 that *"In the beginning was the Word, and the Word was with God, and the Word was God"* Later, *the Word was made flesh and dwells among us.* Paul also reiterated the same fact in Colossians 1:16,*17* that *"For by him were all things created, that are in heaven, and that are in Earth, visible and invisible whether they be thrones, or dominions, or principalities, or powers: all things were created by him, and for him. And he is before all things, and by him all things consist".* So, we know that Jesus was with God even when God was creating the heavens and the Earth. Actually, **he was the Lamb that was slain from the foundation of the world** (Rev. 13:8). But humanity did not encounter Jesus until after the fall of Adam when God prophesied the future redemption of man in Genesis 3:15, *"And I will put enmity between you and the woman, and between your seed and her seed; He shall bruise your head, and you shall bruise his heel".* With this God was announcing that Eve's seed was ultimately going to defeat Satan who has taken away their estate and hijacked their destiny. This seed of the woman referred to Jesus. This was the first time the gospel of Jesus Christ was announced but as a prophecy. Though in that context, it looked like God was talking to the serpent, actually God was talking to Satan that possessed the serpent. You see, the devil is also a spirit being, you can only see him in his manifestations and not with the natural eyes. While God saw Satan in the serpent, because

God is Spirit, Adam and Eve saw only the serpent. The statement was directed to Satan. And that was the only hint that God gave concerning the plan to redeem man, the rest of the plan was planned in secret. The devil did not get the real meaning of this, and God did not intend that the devil knows his intentions and the details; actually God intended it to be a secret plan. God used this statement to initiate the plan of redemption. God had to change His focus concerning man because man could no more exercise dominion over the works of His hands and could no longer replenish the earth as He had planned; instead the devil now had dominion over man, and replenishing the earth with evil, and can now rule man with the power that God gave to man to rule over the devil himself.

Five

THE ENEMY IS RELENTLESS

The devil was also ignorant with the rest of the world about when Jesus was going to come. He got to know that the Messiah had been born through the Angels in the manger and the wise men that came to visit Jesus. This knowledge stirred him up to organize a massacre that would

> It was a battle of words, intentions and purpose. Adam and Eve lost it once and got us all into the trouble that Jesus came to fix. But glory is to God! Jesus won.

kill all male children through King Herod; the ultimate goal was to kill baby Jesus. But God was a step ahead to have initiated Joseph's escape to Egypt with Mary and baby Jesus. Evidently Satan thought that Jesus died with the rest of the innocent children that were killed during that bloody massacre he organized through King Herod. It was a surprise to him one day to see the heavens open, and the Spirit descended upon Jesus like a dove and a voice from heaven announced that *"Thou art my beloved Son, in whom I am well pleased"* – (Matthew 3:17). This sent a strong signal to the kingdom of darkness. Reacting to this, Satan was very curious to know more about Jesus just like he felt when he first discovered Adam and Eve. He just heard the voice proclaiming Jesus as the Son of God. He followed Jesus to the wilderness to find out what he was made up of. He challenged Jesus about his identity saying ***"If you are the Son of God command that these stones be made bread"*** – (Matthew 4:3). It is not a coincident that this was the very first temptation that was put through to Jesus. Satan wanted to know if Jesus actually knew who he was or maybe he could still be manipulated and deceived and he wanted to find out if he can still erode the efficacy of his ministry like he did with Adam and Eve in the Garden of Eden. He tried to incapacitate Jesus.

Now, let us draw significant attention to the second and third temptations to which Jesus responded ***"Thou shall not tempt the Lord thy God"*** - (Matthew 4:7) and ***"Get thee hence Satan: For it is written, Thou shall worship the Lord thy God, and Him only shall you serve"*** – (Matthew 4:10). This account went down in history and it was a vital step for the success of God's redemptive plan. The whole heaven had been waiting for this hour. The devil's strategy of deception and manipulation has just failed. He tried it with Adam and won, now he wanted to do it again with Jesus. The Kingdom of God cannot afford to lose this battle the second time because it would constitute a major setback to the plans of God. Jesus was the only one at the fore front of the battle and his victory was anticipated. It was a battle of words, intentions and purpose. Adam and Eve lost it once and got us all into the trouble that Jesus came to fix. But glory is to God! Jesus won. The whole heaven watched Jesus defeat the devil by the word of God and heard him call himself the devil's God. And I could feel relief in heaven. Here Jesus evidently set in motion the process of taking back what the devil took away from Adam. The devil made a very big mistake; he had just shown Jesus all the kingdoms of the world, the glory, and the hidden riches held in the dark region of the earth. All these Jesus would take back from the devil. Had Jesus fallen, the whole strategies planned for so many years in the secret place would have failed. The devil's coup d'état would have been successful the second time.

That day, the devil must have left the wilderness threatened that he was losing his position. Imagine he must have said to himself "In my entire walk on Earth, no man had ever resisted me like this man Jesus, from Adam to Abraham, to Isaac, to Jacob, to Moses, to David, to Solomon. Did you hear what he said? He said *"Thou shall not tempt the Lord thy God"*. Oh! I thought it would be easy just like it was with Adam". The devil was threatened. He feared that he was losing his position as the ace of the world, a position he had enjoyed for the past four thousand years. What shall I do now? The devil asked himself; Yes, I have an idea, why not just plot against him and use his own words against him, cause darkness in the minds of the people, make His word offend the people, and get the people to kill him so that the kingdom of darkness can lay a claim on his life and he will join us in hell. It sounded a good idea to the devil and his cohorts.

In reaction to Jesus' victory over him in the wilderness, the devil started planning strategies to kill Jesus or discourage Him from fulfilling his mission. One of Satan's strategies was to possess human beings and use them against Jesus. He planned some distractions using the Pharisees so that they might entangle Jesus in his talk (Matthew 22:15-21). He used the Sadducees and scribes to attack Jesus, questioning him on issues like Sabbath, Resurrection, and Marriage with the purpose of getting him into trouble. Also he used rejection by the Jews to discourage him. But Jesus was so focused that he could not be distracted.

The familiar incident where Peter who was a disciple of Jesus was used by the devil to rebuke Jesus against going to the cross is also relevant here, (Mark 8:31-33). For Jesus, going to the cross was God's ordained purpose before he came to this world.

Matthew 16:22-23, *"Then Peter took him, and began to rebuke him, saying, be it far from thee, Lord: this shall not be unto thee. But Jesus turned, and said unto Peter, "Get thee behind me, Satan: thou art an offence unto me: for you savor not the things that be of*

God, but those that be of men". Please take note that this is similar to what he told the devil in the wilderness.

We could see that Jesus recognized the manifestation of Satan in Peter, and Jesus rightly addressed it, just as if Satan was standing physically in front of him.

Moreover, Satan also used Judas Iscariot to betray him, gentiles to scourge him and eventually nailed him to the cross and the devil thought that was the end. But all these did not move Jesus because the more the devil plotted against him, the more Jesus came closer to accomplishing His goals. Unknowingly to the devil, death on the cross was Jesus' goal on the earth. If Jesus did not die on the cross, his purpose was not yet accomplished. This does not mean that God needed the devil to carry out His purpose here on Earth, but the devil always contends with God and wants to stand in God's way at all times. Unfortunately, God cannot be stopped from achieving His purposes. God always has His plans figured out from the beginning, but the devil in the bid to maintain his status quo and out of a spirit of rivalry and jealousy always attempts to disrupt God's plans by taking actions that would cause God's plans to fail. But Romans 8:28 says **"And we know that all things work together for good to them that love God, to them who are the called according to his purpose".** God has made His plan and the devil cannot prevail against it and whatever the devil does to stop it will even act as a catalyst that speeds up the process. The devil out of his own ignorance thinks he's at war with God. Even this imaginary battle, the devil really wanted to win too much.

Jesus had his mind focused so much on the throne of God and the glory that was to follow after his lifetime. So, Jesus' three and a half years ministry were years of focusing on his purpose. Jesus ruled the earth. The devil trembled wherever Jesus was. Jesus could do anything he wanted, he went about doing good, healing the sick, raised the dead, walked on water, calmed the sea, drove out demons, and the devil could do nothing about it. Luke 6:18-19 says it all ***"And they that were vexed with unclean spirits were healed. And the whole multitude sought to touch him; for there went virtue out of him and healed them all"***. He was master of the sea and wind because he commanded them. He was also a master to the one who thought he was the god of this world, the devil. In summary Jesus did here on earth what God intended Adam to do. He had dominion.

Six

THE SOURCE AND DESTINATION

A solemn event took place in heaven; Jesus was about to depart from the Father in heaven to come to the world to fulfill his assignment. He submitted to the will of the Father and said *"Look Father, according to the volume of the book written about me, I have come to do your will - (Hebrew 10:5).* Jesus was going to lay down

> God always has His plans figured out from the beginning, but the devil in the bid to maintain his status quo, and out of a spirit of rivalry and jealousy always attempts to disrupt God's plans by taking actions that he thinks will cause God's plans to fail.

all his glory in heaven and get into the physical human body that God had prepared for him and be subjected to like passion as human beings. He was fashioned so that he would suffer and taste death for every human being that ever comes to this world. This was clear to him before he came. Jesus was leaving the presence of the Father where he was royalty and enjoyed everything for the earth where he would be harassed and confronted and finally would be condemned to death as a criminal. This was a risk. But Jesus was willing to take this risk despite the fact that he knew it was not going to be easy.

Let us look at the following statement which was made by Jesus when he was here on earth. It is actually a prophecy expressing what will happen to him in the nearest future according to the mandate given to him by the Father.

Behold, we go up to the Jerusalem; and the son of man shall be betrayed unto the chief priests and unto the scribes, and they shall condemn him to death. And shall deliver him to the Gentiles to mock, and to scourge, and to crucify him; and the third day he shall rise again. (Matthew 20:18, 19)

Now, imagine that this same statement was made in heaven just before he left the father, it would have read "**Behold we go down to the Earth; and the son of man** *shall be betrayed unto the chief priests and unto the scribes, and they shall condemn him to death. And shall deliver him to the Gentiles to mock, and to scourge, and to crucify him; and the third day he shall rise again.*"

This would then be a summary of the life of Jesus just before he left heaven for the earth till the time he was resurrected from death. It is a three part statement and each part would be explained based on the executor. This statement is in line with John 16:28 that *"I came from the Father, and am come into the world: again, I leave the world, and go to the Father".* The Father was both the source and the destination.

There is no gainsaying that Jesus in heaven was aware of the details of the life he would live and the suffering he would go through here on earth before he left God the Father in heaven. He knew exactly why He was coming and how he was going to come into this world like a traveler is aware of details of his itinerary.

The Father was both the source and the destination because he said, I came from the Father and in the end he said I go to the Father. This means that God was the originator of the journey and God was the destination because Jesus would return to the Father with a note of completion of his assignment in his hands. This was why Jesus lived a purpose driven life. He focused on the one reason why he was sent to this world. He did not allow anything to get him out of focus. By the time you finish reading this book, there should be no misunderstanding about the mission, purpose and personality of Jesus and why God chose him to do His most crucial work here on earth.

Jesus Started The Journey

The first section of the statement, *"We go up to Jerusalem"* translates to *"We go down to the Earth"* in our context. This was carried out by Jesus himself. He had to agree to be the lamb to be slain, he had to leave all His glory in heaven and come to the World as a man, composing himself in the nature of a man.

"And the Word was made flesh and dwelt among us…" John 1:14

He had to humble himself and be born as a baby, he knew that he was going to suffer alone, betrayed and denied by friends, he would have to overcome the human weakness and fear of pain, all these He knew even before He came to the world and came to terms with them. In real life here on earth, Jesus knew he would have to accommodate the contention of the Scribes and Pharisees. He had to work against the flesh in these circumstances and allow His spirit to take the lead; because the flesh resisted him, and at the height of his ministry on earth he said *"The spirit is willing but the flesh is weak"*. He had to pray alone with no one supporting him though he could have used some help from Peter, James and John who could not watch with him but fell asleep.

Later Jesus was praying in the garden of Gethsemane, he saw the multitude of sin, diseases and pain that would be placed upon him on the cross, he cried *"O Father, if thou be willing, remove this cup from me: nevertheless not my will, but yours, be done"*. That is a cognitive restructuring of phrase which he used to override his own human will. Here Jesus was exhibiting the human side of him; this tells us that the pain he was to go through was real; he was not going to receive any anesthesia. This proves to us that he had the same emotion as we do. I can feel and hear God saying – "Oh Son, I wish we could do it another way, but you are the only perfect sacrifice that can restore and redeem mankind. Beside, we have both waited for four thousand years for this hour, now we cannot change the plan because there is no other way to do it. Just be strong and of good courage". And the bible says in Luke 22:43, "And there appeared an Angel unto him from heaven, strengthening him". God was making the captain of our salvation perfect through suffering.

He said in John 12:27 that *"Now is my soul troubled; and what shall I say? Father, save me from this hour: but for this cause I came to this hour".* These are statements that make us appreciate the pains he went through in order to reconcile us to God.

The Devil Caused Confusion

The middle part *"and the son of man shall be betrayed unto the chief priests and unto the scribes, and they shall condemn him to death. And shall deliver him to the Gentiles to mock, and to scourge, and to crucify him"* was carried out by Satan. Remember that Satan was extremely slighted when Jesus refused his temptation? He immediately started planning a payback for Jesus.

Satan saw Jesus and thought God must have made a big mistake by sending Jesus to the world in the flesh because he thought no man in the flesh can escape his dominion. Already, Satan was king in the physical world, and the physical human body is already under his control, so he thought he would have control over Jesus' physical body as well. The devil saw divinity inside of humanity and thought if he can deceive and defeat the physical human body of Jesus like he did for Adam, he can capture the divinity on the inside. The devil therefore took Jesus to an exceeding high mountain and tried to nullify the divinity inside of him by persuading Jesus to worship him while offering him kingdoms and glory in return; knowingly well that to God, worship is key and it must be done in spirit and in truth. Who you worship, you shall obey. Jesus had already obeyed the Father; to obey Satan as well would be a sacrilegious compromise. But thanks be to God, Jesus was able to turn the table around and set the record straight by telling the devil to worship him instead. Despite all the devil's attempts to get him distracted from his primary assignment here on earth, Jesus remained focused, and undistracted. Applaud Jesus!!!

The devil possessed Judas Iscariot to betray Jesus Christ. John 13:27 says *"And after the sop Satan entered into him. Then Jesus said unto him, that you are going to do, do it quickly".* Jesus always recognized the manifestation of the devil at the very first appearance. It might appear to all that Jesus was talking to Judas, but Jesus was actually talking to the devil that already possessed Judas. The devil also set the Pharisees, scribes and the high priests against Jesus and made Pilate scourge him and condemn him without a reason.

John 19:6b says *"Pilate said unto them, Take him, and crucify him: for I find no fault in him".* Does that statement make any sense at all? Later in John 19:16, Pilate delivered him unto the people to be crucified. When Pilate found no fault in him why did he not set him free and let him go? The devil was controlling his judgment. But Jesus made a timely pronouncement that knocks the devil on his head and says it all in John 19:11 *"You could have no power at all against me, except it was given you from above; therefore he that delivered me unto you has greater sin".* That part that says *"he that delivered me unto you has greater sin"* refers to Satan.

The devil also made the Jews to prefer Barabbas the murderer to Jesus, and made the chief priest and officers to shout "**crucify him**" when they were asked by Pilate to choose between Jesus and

Barabbas, they chose Barabbas. This was a corporate manifestation of the act of the devil upon the chief priest, officers, scribes and the Pharisees and the people. You could feel it at the background and their deceived minds. In actual fact they did not know what they were doing, even Jesus acknowledged that fact when he was about to give up the ghost. The devil was the culprit here, he blinded their eyes and the onus is on him. It brings some relief to know that the people did not actually know what they were doing. Satan's involvement in orchestrating the crucifixion of Jesus was rightfully depicted in the Passion of the Christ movie where you see Satan at the background of all the revolts against Jesus, and it rightly tells who exactly killed Jesus. It was not really strange that Jesus had to pray to the father on behalf of those who nailed him to the cross that the father should forgive them because they did not know what they were doing. This was because Jesus knew that it was the devil that blinded them. All these happened that the scriptures might be fulfilled. They thought they were conspiring against the man that violated their custom. They thought they were crucifying the man that committed blasphemy by claiming to be the Son of God.

They did not know that it was the devil that instigated them against Jesus just for the purpose of keeping his position as the god of this world.

Even Caiaphas the high priest was deceived in the bid to protect the traditional religion of Judaism, he despised Jesus. The point is that Satan can invade the soul realm and cause confusion through deception.

And God The Father Fulfilled His Promise

Someone would say "And God the Father gets the touchdown!". In American Football, the touchdown is worth 6 points. It is scored when a player catches a pass or runs the ball in his opponent's end zone.

The last action "And **the third day he shall rise again**" was orchestrated by God himself, and it was a touchdown. Note that Jesus trusted the Father unto death.

God the Father sustained Jesus till the end even in his darkest moment the spirit of Jesus was quickened. Jesus went into the enemy's camp and wrought a mighty victory just because God was there to sustain him otherwise the story would have been different. If God decided not to raise Jesus up, he would be dead forever. On that cross, Jesus was drained of all strength and power and the best he could do was to rely on God for everything including his resurrection. This was why it was critical that everything that Jesus did while he was in the world was satisfactory to God; that guarantees that the travail of Jesus' soul satisfied God and that Jesus was a perfect sacrifice.

We also see the faithfulness of God demonstrated by fulfilling His promise to His Son Jesus. The prophecy was pronounced through King David that *"For you will not leave my soul in hell; neither will you suffer your Holy One to see corruption"* (Psalm 16:10), and the prophecy was finally reinforced by Jesus when he was about to die that *"Father, unto your hands do I commend my spirit"* (Luke 23:46). And on the third day God sent the power of resurrection to raise him up from the dead, and Jesus was able to use that same power to defeat the devil and took back what he had stolen from mankind. Jesus later ascended to heaven to report to God that the mission has been accomplished.

All Jesus could think about was the glory that would follow after the suffering on the cross. Even-though, the suffering on the cross was going to be very painful, he was willing to go through it because he knew that after all the suffering there is glory awaiting him. He said *"And now Father, glorify thou me with your own self with the glory which I had with you before the world was"*. *(John 17:5)*, also in Hebrew 12:2 says *"Looking unto Jesus the author and finisher of our faith who for the joy that was set before him endured the cross, despising the shame, and is set down at the right hand of the throne of God."*

God fulfilled all his promises. The book of Philippians 2: 9-11 says *"Wherefore God also hath highly exalted him, and given him a name which is above every name. That at the name of Jesus every knee should bow, of things in heaven, and things under the earth; And that every tongue should confess that Jesus Christ is Lord, to the glory of God the Father"*.

In summary, this tells us that God is in control of the affairs of humanity, and he's the architect. He knows the end from the beginning and even if it looks like the devil is gaining an upper-hand, it does not matter to God because the devil keeps digging his own grave with every of his actions.

Sometimes the action of the devil is critical to the success of God's plan, not that God planned it that way but because the devil wants God to fail, he takes some actions which otherwise would have been disastrous to God's plan but for that particular purpose, such actions have been ordained to contribute positively to the plans of God. As you read this book, you would see how one of such actions of Satan accelerated the plan of God in the life of Jesus. God's plan will never fail; He always has the victory in the end. People who think the devil is winning the battle are making a big mistake. The devil is just marking time, he's not making any progress, and he's just getting better at doing what he does best because he's been doing it for too long. He cannot invent the wheel or shift the envelope of wisdom because it is God's project, only God can. He cannot create on his own; he only imitates what God has done and capitalizes on it. He will continue doing this until God initiates the next level in the chain of events.

Seven

PRESERVED BY RIGHTEOUSNESS

The cross was the last event in the life of Jesus that the natural man could relate to because the rest of the events happened in the spiritual realm; only the new creation, spirit filled person can understand and believe it.

> God's eyes had always been on Jesus but now he would have to turn away. The life that used to flow between them would seize

Humanity would still be under the dominion of the kingdom of darkness if God did not send the power of resurrection to raise Jesus from the dead. Humanity would still be unsaved, un-forgiven and dominated by the devil if Jesus is not seated by the right hand of God after the blood of Jesus was presented to God.

God was satisfied with the sacrifice of Jesus on the cross so, Jesus was able to seat at the right hand of God. The bible says in Isaiah 53:11 that *"He shall see of the travail of his soul and shall be satisfied".* If there had been any sin in Jesus' life while he was here on earth, his name would have been forgotten because the cross would have been his last event and it would have been a mere suffering with no results because God is no respecter of person. What took Jesus **beyond the**

cross was righteousness. Hell could not pin any sin on him. And that was why he was justified in the spirit.

2 Corinthians 5:21 says ***"For He hath made him to be sin for us, who knew no sin; that we might become the righteousness of God in Him"***

Without justification there would have been no resurrection and without resurrection there would have been no redemption. It was done for love so that we could go beyond sin and death and not get stuck in the darkness of the physical realm.

The status of the redemption plan at this time was good. God had his plan in place and so far everything was going on as planned. The devil will now work out its own destruction.

God knew what Satan could do in order to protect his position and place. All that God was waiting for was that Jesus should gain access to hell as a sinner and God knew that Satan would take the spirit of Jesus there in order to secure his position here on earth. Once this happens, the success of God's redemptive plan is assured.

God knew He was going to suffer as well. God's suffering would come when he would turn his face away from Jesus because he could not behold the magnitude of sin that has been put on Him. God's eyes had always been on Jesus but now he would have to turn away. The life that used to flow between them would seize.

There was a period of separation between God the Father and Jesus His son; this was the time God the Father could not behold the sin that was laid upon Jesus anymore and turned His face away from Jesus. At that time Jesus cried to the Father and said "Eli, Eli, lama sabachthani?" That was a question meaning My God, My God, why have you forsaken me? Before this statement was made by Jesus, there was a period of great physical darkness between the sixth and the ninth hour. Even the Sun and the moon responded to the countenance of God. This period of darkness signified a painful and depressing time for God the Father but then, it was the time when God left His son to suffer on the cross and extended salvation to other nations apart from the Jews. It was the time according to the time-table of heaven when God did the actual sowing of his seed in form of His son Jesus to reap a multitude of people. It was the prime time for the actual investment to take place. The period of sowing is always very difficult especially when the seed is an expensive one. God's countenance was changed because His suffering Son was dying alone on the cross and God had to cut away all connection with him at that time. The triune God-head was working together towards the same goal but they had to work apart from each other.

God's greatest despise of His Son Jesus on the cross led to God's greatest affinity towards humanity. The exchange was so phenomenal no one could imagine.

The tone at that period expressed a mutual pain between the Father and His Son. And this was the time that the actual substitution took place.

God left His Son on the cross and reached out to the entire human race. Jesus was neglected so that humanity could be embraced. He became poor so that we could be rich. He was whipped with stripes, and stricken with diseases so that we might be healed. This was the hardest time of God's existence ever, but God was prepared to go through this for the sake of mankind. So, not only did Jesus suffer for man's redemption but God the Father also suffered. God did not just sit on His throne looking at Jesus suffering on the cross. He was also busy doing and perfecting the work of redemption. At the same time, and at the death of Jesus, the veil of the temple was torn from top to bottom signifying that the barrier between God and humanity has been removed and that not only the high priest can approach God but everyone. Also that there is no more need for animal sacrifice but the perfect sacrifice of Jesus is enough for atonement.

Hebrew 2:14

Forasmuch then as the children are partakers of flesh and blood, he also himself likewise took part of the same; that through death he might destroy him that had the power of death, that is the devil; and deliver them who through fear of death were all their lifetime subject to bondage.

God knew that if Jesus died physically on the cross and is taken to hell, which by nature cannot contain him because his spiritual nature is different and therefore they cannot co-exist. God also knew He was going to pour His great power on Jesus, and he was going to be raised up by this great power that the devil cannot withstand. This great power is called the power of resurrection.

The next stage was that Jesus should gain access to hell as a sinner. Nobody but the devil can do this because up till this time, Satan held the key of death and hell. So, at a certain stage, to jeer him up, Jesus told the devil appearing as Judas in John 13:27 *"What you are going to do, do quickly"*. The bible says no man at the table knew what Jesus meant. They could not understand because Jesus discerned it spiritually, but Satan understood because he knew the work he was doing inside Judas. They saw Judas but Jesus saw Satan in Judas who was actually possessed of Satan. In response to that Judas left the room to consult with the conspirators who wanted Jesus crucified. The person of Judas would not do this by himself but he did it because he was possessed of Satan. Judas did not know what he was doing at this time. But this is not an argument to support Judas' person because he made himself susceptible to the devil through his love and greed for money in the first place.

The next event is even more exciting, *"Therefore, when Judas was gone out, Jesus said, Now is the Son of man glorified, and God glorified in him. If God be glorified in him, God shall also glorify him in himself, and shall straightway glorify him"*(John 13:31).

Notice that Jesus did not say this when Judas was still in the room with him, he made sure that Judas left the room because at that time the devil was actually in Judas. Remember, the mission of redemption was planned in secret, so, Satan must not be aware of it at this time. What Jesus was implying was like "Yes, the wheel has now been set in motion; the time of glorification has come". It sounded like Jesus was excited about it, at this time he was not thinking about the suffering on the cross because the joy of glorification surpassed the suffering on the cross, and that he knew he was fulfilling the perfect will of God. Still Jesus did not want Satan to hear that his action would bring glory to him because that part of the plan was still a secret. If Satan knew that Jesus would be glorified after suffering, he might put a halt to his crucifixion plans which was actually God's target for Jesus.

Hebrew 12:2

Looking unto Jesus the author and finisher of our faith; who for the joy that was set before him endured the cross, despising the shame, and is set down at the right hand of the throne of God.

When Jesus was suffering on the cross, those that claimed to love him and believed in Him cried and were disappointed that he was dying just because they did not know what God was achieving. Even the disciples whom Jesus had told about the impending event had forgotten that it was written in the scriptures that Jesus must suffer and die. Peter and John were looking at Him from a distance; Peter did not want to be associated with Him for fear of the Jews. There would have being some relief in the air if someone had remembered at that time that all these had been foretold in the scriptures. Most of them were expecting Jesus to perform a miracle and free himself from the cross at the last minute. They were not expecting Him to die. So, they were disappointed that Jesus was dying on the cross. The devil had blinded their imaginations corporately. They actually did not know what they were doing just like Jesus said on the cross. But all these happened so that the plan of God - the scripture, might be fulfilled.

Eight

A SNARE FOR THE FOWLER

A trap has now been set for the trapper himself. Usually, it is the fowler that sets snares for people but this time, a snare was planned for the fowler himself and he was going to fall badly and no one was going to fore-warn him.

The plan was that Jesus should suffer on the cross, and then his spirit man be taken to hell, while in hell, he would take back what the devil took from Adam. In the

> Since Satan was the one holding the key of death and hell he thought he had the right to imprison mankind in hell. Now he wants to do it again, this time for the holy one of God, Jesus Christ.

process of achieving this, the devil would use his zeal for survival to make this plan possible. The devil meant evil for Jesus and having desired too much to retain his position as the prince of this world, all of his wicked steps were programmed to be the very thing that will make God's redemptive plan possible. Jesus' steps were ordered by God and all things worked together for good for him because he was in the world to fulfill God's purpose.

Jesus knew quite well that he has come to this world to seek and save that which was lost through Adam, and preserve lives by a great deliverance, so if Jesus wanted to fulfill his mission here on earth he must put himself in a condition whereby he would be able to do that. He upheld the integrity of his authority and did not compromise. He overwhelmed the kingdom of darkness and proved that they were underneath his feet.

All the sufferings that Jesus endured were part of the process of seeking that which was lost. He had to be careful, gentle and humble otherwise he would not have been able to find that purpose talk less of saving it. He was a Director but had to be a cleaner in the smaller branch of the Creation Investment Corporation for a period of time. This way, the competitors will see him as one of the cleaners, and treat him that way, not knowing that he had the skills, ability and nature of a director in him. They see him as humanity but he has divinity inside of him.

The event on the cross goes a long way to tell us more about the character of God. He will continue with His plans even if mankind does not understand or see the reason for it. He does not want to flex his muscle and prove to us what he can do. Jesus would have prayed to the Father to provide him with twelve legions of Angels to fight on his behalf; if this had happened, the scripture would not be fulfilled. He said *"**Nobody takes my life from me but I laid down my life and will pick it up again"**.* He was acting in faith. He was focused, and knew what he was doing and why. God the Father did not force him to do it, but he would submit himself to the suffering on the cross.

This was a man who was supposed to be their Messiah, but on the cross, he was dying helplessly. The Jews even thought something was going to happen at the last moment, but he died. The devil was joyous he thought that was the end. He was happy because the man that amazed and astonished him for the past three years has finally been silenced and now he can continue to reign wickedly. The man that walked on water, rebuked the storm, fed the multitude, healed the impotent, raised the dead, overwhelmed and proved to be a terror to the kingdom of darkness was about to die shamefully on the cross. What a joy this brought to Satan.

Satan was at that time the holder of the keys of hell and death. He knew who came in and who went out. He was the one that laid claim on any dead human being and qualified them as candidates of hell; and he did this based on the sin found in and on them because sin was the basis of spiritual death. Sin was the sting of death, and death was the wages of sin. These were all formulated by Satan because God did not have any plan for death. God's plan for mankind was eternal life.

Moreover, the most exciting thing in the world history was about to happen. The devil was about to lay claim on Jesus' spirit just like he contended for Moses after he died but was with-held by Angel Michael who simply said "The Lord rebuke you" as reported in Jude 1:9. This time, no angel was going to withhold the devil, but this was for a reason. Since Satan was the one holding the key of death and hell he thought he had the right to imprison mankind in hell. Now he wanted to do it again, this time for the holy one of God, Jesus Christ. Just Watch this! Remember Jesus had already prophesied that *"The prince of this world comes and has nothing in me"* - John 14:30; in contrary to that, on this fateful day, after Jesus gave up the ghost, Satan found lots and lots of sin and diseases on Jesus. The devil sensed sin on Jesus and quickly qualified him as a candidate of hell without wondering where the sin came from. Remember the devil was not aware of God's plan to lay the sins of the whole human race on Jesus. Satan was surprised to see so much diseases and sin on Jesus and wondered why he did not know about Jesus' sinfulness. As a result of this, the spirit of Jesus was taken to hell to be imprisoned because he was made sin. This stage was critical to the plan because Jesus would not have been able to gain access to hell by his righteous and holy self; he needed sin and spiritual death to get him there; so that when Satan conducts his spot check he will find sin on him and qualify him as a candidate of hell. What Satan did not know was that the sin and diseases he saw on Jesus' spirit belonged to all mankind past, present and future and that it was God's doing. It was God himself that planned it so that the sin of the world would be laid on Jesus as a vital part of the strategy, so that Satan can have a reason to lay claim on Jesus' spirit and imprison him in hell. The mere fact that Jesus was crucified on the cross brought curses on him. It was in fulfillment of the requirements of God's law that says the cursed one should hang on the tree. So, the incidental hanging of Christ was a confirmation that the curse on humanity was laid on Christ while on the cross. This satisfied the strict and righteous demands of God's holy law. Jesus also used this occasion to abolish that law, the handwriting of ordinances that were written against us, and brought life and immortality to light - **(Colossians 2:14, 2 Timothy 1:10)**

At this point, the devil was convinced that since he found sin on Jesus, he could rightfully take him to hell. Moreover, Jesus' spirit was eventually taken to hell but unknowingly to the devil, the multitude of sin, diseases, and curses remained on the cross with Jesus' body, they were nailed to the cross of Calvary, and shortly after, the holy and righteous spirit of Jesus was taken to hell.

Colossians 2:14

"Blotting out the handwriting of ordinances that was against us, which was contrary to us, and took it out of the way, nailing it to his cross"

And God knew that whatever was laid upon Jesus at crucifixion will not stick on him **beyond the cross** but will all be nailed to the cross.

So, unknowingly to the devil, Jesus' spirit entered into hell without sin. Jesus entered into hell with an innocent, holy and righteous spirit. This state is dangerous for the kingdom of darkness. The devil overlooked this righteousness in Jesus, shifted emphasis on the sin of the whole world that were put on Jesus, qualified him as a candidate in hell and made a mistake of his life, a mistake that he would ever live to regret. No one messes with the righteousness of God in Christ Jesus. It is too hot to handle. It can even cause an explosion; and it did cause an explosion in hell.

At this time the heavens rejoiced that Jesus has finally reached his destination according to the master plan.

On the other side, Satan and his cohorts in hell, unaware of what God had planned, were at this time rejoicing for victory over the son of God that they had imprisoned.

The stage is now set for God to put completion into the redemptive plan of man. The next event in the sequence of planning is now to be orchestrated by God himself. God knew that if Jesus died physically, the devil cannot withstand Him in the spiritual realm, because that is the real realm where Jesus is the only King. Hebrews 2:14 ***"Forasmuch then as the children are partakers of flesh and blood, he also himself likewise took part of the same; that through death he might destroy him that had the authority of death, that is the devil".***

And finally God intervened

The spirit of Jesus must still suffer in hell for three days and three nights according to the master plan; and this period was to be used to meet the demands of Justice and paying the wages that bought us back as God's purchased possession. Jesus at this time became the prisoner to be punished for the sins committed by me. Right there on the cross, the greatest exchange took place. And my name changed. My identity changed as God unleashed the fury of His anger on Jesus. Once he gets to hell to suffer for sin and serves his term, God shall see the travail of his soul, and shall be satisfied. Then mankind would be forgiven and sin would loosen its grip on humanity and the punishment imposed through death would expire, and grace would be poured out.

"Yet it pleased the Lord to bruise him; he hath put him to grief: when you shall make his soul an offering for sin, he shall see his seed, he shall prolong his days, and the pleasure of the Lord shall prosper in his hand. He shall see of the travail of his soul, and shall be satisfied" - Isaiah 53:10, 11.

Once God was satisfied by the travail of his soul in hell and He can equate that to the redemption of humanity, then that's all that matters; because God was the one offended by the disobedience of Adam and not Satan who was one of the perpetrators or instigators. God is the one that would determine the extent of suffering that would justify our redemption. **"It is God that justifies"** – Romans 8:33.

Because Jesus suffered on the cross and subsequently suffered silently in hell, he met all the claims that the accuser held against humanity; a prisoner who completely served his sentence and would be free afterwards. In his death he partook of Satan's nature, the sinful nature, because he died spiritually and sin was found on him and not in him. When Jesus was justified, humanity was forgiven.

"For He made Him who knew no sin to be sin for us, that we might become the righteousness of God in Him." *(2 Corinthians 5:21).* And Isaiah 53:6b gave the same prophecy that *"and the Lord hath laid on him the iniquity of us all".*

After a period of seventy-two hours of suffering in hell, God's eyes were set upon His son, Jesus; and He said "that is it". Up until now, the third Director – God the Holy Spirit had been patiently waiting to rush in to aid Jesus out of the situation but had to wait until he gets a go ahead from God the Father. Immediately he got the green light, he rushed into the heart of hell where Jesus' spirit was laying and quickened him. The spirit of Jesus then started to glow with extremely bright light and radiance, an occurrence that never happened in hell before. The light of God in the midst of the darkness of the pit of hell definitely made Satan and his demons to scream and shout out in defeat. The light was intended to torment them. These lights were the invisible lights operating in their individual frequencies according to the electromagnetic spectrum. They range from Gamma rays to X-rays, to ultraviolet. Remember, God is the Father of lights. Jesus' spirit started radiating with different kinds of light. When they think they have had enough another light would reveal itself, and they were tormented the more. It was like sustained fireworks, an atomic bomb that caused an explosion. The power of resurrection was at work in Jesus in hell.

In our Creation Investment Corporation analogy, this time means "No more undercover operations, now is the time to show up as a Director". This also means a switch of his role from the **Lamb that was slain** to the **Lion of Judah** that confronted the devil and took back the power, spoilt principalities and powers and made a public parade of them. And said "Lift up your heads O ye gates; and be ye lifted up, ye everlasting doors; and the King of glory shall come in. The enemy who still had not yet realized how much trouble was looming around him asked "Who is this King of glory?" And an angel replied "The Lord, strong and mighty, the Lord mighty in battle, The Lord of hosts, he is the King of glory.

At this stage, Jesus then confronted the devil with this great power of resurrection that the devil cannot withstand. Satan must have been extremely surprised to see Jesus' spirit quickened. So Jesus demanded the POWER that he stole from Adam back in the Garden of Eden. Satan could not resist because he could not withstand Jesus who came with great power, and besides, this caught him unawares since he was not expecting the spirit of Jesus to be quickened. Satan did not have any alternative but to surrender to Jesus all the power he stole from Adam. **Remember: Had he known he would not have crucified the king of glory**. Also remember that **Jesus was the sacred secret weapon of God**...

Jesus was delivered for our offences, and was raised again for our justification. "And without controversy, great is the mystery of godliness: God was manifest in the flesh, justified in the spirit". It is important to know that Jesus was justified in the spirit after our sins were forgiven. The power of resurrection has a quickening ability that brings a condemned spirit to life after the spirit has been exonerated from sin. Jesus was justified and made alive in the spirit.

Jesus possessed the gates of hell by going into Satan's territory to wrought victory over him in the very place where Satan had his stronghold. And the bible says in Colossians 2:16 *"Having spoiled principalities and powers, he made a public show of them openly, triumphing over them in it".* This is why Satan will always bow at the mention of the name of Jesus.

Public Shows and the triumphs

The devil thought he had the victory when Jesus was suffering on the cross; he exposed Jesus to an open shame in the presence of a couple of thousand people and thought he had wrought a mighty victory. The situation was reversed in the spiritual realm, in hell actually, when Jesus, spoiled principalities and powers and paraded them openly; rendering them harmless and triumphing over them in it.

The devil had his own turn of the public show when Jesus was on the cross, naked, despised and in shame. This was in the physical realm. Satan did this openly so that it may appear to people that Jesus had died and mankind lost again. This made him look good in the kingdom of darkness that they were making progress. Now, the situation would reverse in the spiritual realm where the actual battle would take place. Jesus would have his own turn of public show openly so that it may appear to all in the spirit realm that the devil who had been the king of this world for about four thousand years had been dethroned and rendered powerless and that will forever be a witness against him. This fact would later be revealed to people in the physical world through the Holy Spirit.

Millions of people were there to witness this parade. People who have been held captive in Paradise since the time of Noah witnessed it, Father Abraham seeing Jesus emerged finally received the promise that he saw afar off, even the thief on the right hand during crucifixion made his appointment with Jesus in Paradise and witnessed this scene.

Here we see the power being exchanged again, but this time from Satan to Jesus. So, we are not surprised when Jesus said in Matthew 28:18 that ***"All power is given unto me in heaven and in Earth"***, and in Revelation 1:18, *Jesus said **I am he that lives, and was dead; and, behold, I am alive for ever more, Amen; and have the keys of hell and of death**.*

Basically Jesus took back everything that the devil took from Adam in the Garden of Eden and called them the KEY. This was the moment that God had been waiting for. All heaven was hailing Jesus but Jesus had to fight the battle by himself. Much more activities took place in the spirit realm than the physical realm because it is the actual realm. The physical realm to which humanity can relate is only for manifestation purposes but actual design and execution of events take place in the spiritual realm. The power of resurrection was the power used in quickening the spirit of Jesus and to make him confront the devil and defeat him. This is the actual power of God in the person of God the Holy Spirit. Romans 8:11 says ***"But if the spirit of him that raised Jesus from the dead dwells in you, he that raised up Christ from the dead shall also quicken your mortal bodies by his Spirit that dwells in you"***. This power of resurrection is the same power that dwells within us. In Ephesians 3:19, the bible says ***"Now unto him who is able to do exceeding abundantly above all that we ask or think, according to the power that works in us"***. The power that works in us is the power of resurrection and that is the ability that overcomes the devil and makes God to answer our prayers according to the measure of it. So, we are always sure to overcome the devil every time as long as we abide in Christ. ***Whereunto I also labor, striving according to his working, which works in me mightily*** (Colossians 1:29) .

Crucifixion comes before resurrection. Resurrection comes after God is pleased with your crucifixion. There is no resurrection without crucifixion. Crucifixion provides death to the sinful nature while resurrection provides life to the power of God in us.

Nine

THE SECRET WEAPON OF GOD

God had a plan but before the plan there was a purpose. There would have been no reason for the plan but the purpose was betrayed by Adam's non-compliance to the instructions given to him by God thereby yielding to the negative persuasions of Satan thereby selling his inheritance to the enemy of God and changing the course of history. The plan was God's remedy that would eventually connect humanity back to eternity and thereby taking us back to the initial purpose of God. We could see that there was a purpose but there was also a process. The purpose may never be attained if the focus was not clear during the process. The success of Jesus' ministry here on earth is the process needed to bring us back to God's purpose. For Jesus to fulfill this purpose here on earth, he needed an undivided focus.

> God's plan to redeem man was a package and was hidden from the kingdom of darkness so that they will not know "HOW" and "WHEN" God was going to carry out His plan. God planned it for four thousand years and kept it a secret.

What happened in the Garden of Eden was a real **coup d'état** that disrupted God's plan for mankind. God then had to device a careful means of getting things back to normal so that His plan for mankind would still be achieved.

God is able to forcefully put an end to the influence of the devil over man but He is a righteous God and believes in doing things the right way so the devil might not accuse him of using his veto power, and of injustice. He is patient and suffers long. He does not need to flex His muscles and show what he can do but he tarries and does exactly what is meaningful to Him in His time. He works all things out by the counsel of his own will. He knows the end of it all from the beginning and he has prophesied to the devil that his end is destruction and that he would eventually be cast into the lake of fire eternally.

God's intention to redeem man was a program plan that was hidden from the kingdom of darkness so that they would not know "HOW" and "WHEN" God was going to carry out His plan. God planned it for four thousand years and kept it a secret.

1 Corinthians 2:7-8

"But we speak the wisdom of God in a mystery, even the hidden wisdom, which God ordained before the world unto our glory: which none of the princes of this world knew, for had they known it, they would not have crucified the Lord of glory".

A deep understanding of the scripture verse above is required in order to genuinely understand this chapter.

It is necessary to understand that our redemption would not have been achieved if Jesus was not crucified. Also, the power would still be in the hands of the devil if Jesus did not go to hell. Also at this time, the key of hell was in the hand of Satan meaning that no one can go to hell without Satan knowing about it and no mortal being can go to hell without the flesh dying first because hell is only for spirits. Even

Jesus had to die first before his spirit went to hell and this was not without Satan knowing about it.

God intended the plan to be a mystery, and he kept it a secret for four thousand years.

After the historic fall of Adam and Eve in the Garden of Eden, God knew that it will take a man of flesh, blood and bone, born of a woman, who never bowed to the devil to take back the power stolen by the devil. So God conceived the idea that the only way to redeem the earth from the devil was if a physical man who has never yielded to the temptations of the devil could be counted with sinners and be imprisoned in hell. If a righteous person can go to hell, hell by nature will not be able to withstand him. This person can then possess the gates of hell and capture Satan, and take back the power that he stole from Adam. No human being on earth can fit this description, unless if God himself becomes man.

The power was stolen from humanity, so, humanity must take it back and not God; this was why it was Jesus, the Director of Human affairs that was sent to redeem the ill-fated company. Jesus came into the Earth not as God but in form of a man. The bible says that he took not on him the nature of angels, but he took on him the seed of Abraham.

"Forasmuch then as the children are partakers of flesh and blood, he also himself likewise took part of the same, that through death he might destroy him that had the power of death, that is, the devil. And deliver them who through fear of death were all their lifetime subject to bondage. Wherefore in all things it behoved him to be made like unto his brethren, that he might be a merciful and faithful high priest in all things pertaining to God, to make reconciliation for the sins of the people. For, in that he himself hath suffered being tempted; he is able to succor them that are tempted." – Hebrews 2:14-18

In the Creation Investment example, all the attempts made by the Chief Executive Director to redeem this company had failed until He decided that he would have to go by himself. But the tricky part is that he could not go in the office of the Director, however, he must disguise as one of the defeated managers that he originally employed so that the competitors might not recognize him. He must humble himself, enter the city quietly, work as a cleaner just like the other displaced managers for a while until he knows the actual secrets and strengths of the competitors who stole his company from him. This is the undercover operation explained earlier in this book.

This plan was kept a secret because if the devil knew about it, he might prepare himself against the manifestation and might act as a stumbling block. **Jesus was the secret weapon of God against Satan.** One thing about secret weapons is that they are concealed from the enemy until they are ready to be used. For secret weapons to achieve their goals, they must be a surprise to the enemy.

Just like the second coming of Christ is now a mystery to everybody but God, so was the first coming of Christ. Everybody knew the Messiah would be here one day but nobody knew the time he would come, even his mission here on earth was not clearly understood. There were lots of misunderstandings; some thought he would come flying from the sky and declare himself a warrior; but God had another idea. Men could not relate to it when Jesus came as a baby in the manger, a son of a carpenter who had to grow up.

His purpose was also misunderstood as they all thought he was going to save only the Jews from the governance of the Romans but nobody knew He was going to save humanity from the hands of Satan. The Jews thought that the Messiah was sent only to them just like Moses was sent to deliver mainly the Israelites from Egypt. Most of them did not know his purpose until after his death when God's plan was unfolded through the Apostle Paul. This in itself was another mystery.

Jesus said in John 8:36 that *"Him whom the son sets free is free indeed"*. He was going to free their spirits from the kingdom of darkness, but they would not understand. They did not know that God created them a spirit being, they could only see things in the physical realm.

Jesus knew his mission on earth quite well and that was why he said in Luke 19:10 that *"For the Son of man is come to seek and to save that which was lost."*

There is no actual ongoing battle between God and the devil because the devil had been clearly and eternally defeated since the beginning of time, the Supreme Being had been determined and that was God Almighty Himself.

What the devil is doing right now is to get God's attention by causing trouble with the things that interest God. God refers to His children as **"Apple of my eye"**; be rest assured that God knows about it when one of these is in trouble.

"After the glory hath he sent me unto the nations which spoiled you: for he that touches you touched the apple of his eye." - Zachariah 2:8

Let us illustrate this with a typical example of the terrorists who would attack the United States' interests all over the world just because at that time it was impossible for them to hurt the United States directly but they can get the attention of the United States by attacking their interests. These interests are in locations that are not as fortified as the United States herself but they are vulnerable to the attacks of the terrorists. Therefore, whenever they strike, the US government knows about it. God knows about it when you are attacked by His enemy. God knows that the enemy is attacking you in order to get his attention.

Fortifying the interests

If the United States, in a bid to prevent their interests from being attacked, empowers each of their locations all over the world by installing missiles and weaponry so that they can all be self-defensive, the terrorist will have to think twice before they strike. Can you imagine the cost of doing this? It would be in the billions. Despite that cost, God made that kind of investment for you and I. God planted the seed in the form of Jesus and wanted humanity empowered so that they can defend themselves when the devil comes to attack or deceive them. The fruit of this is the empowerment that we find in :-

- Authority in the Name of Jesus - *Strong Tower, Safety, Obtainer*
- The Blood Of Jesus - *Sanctifier*
- The Word Of God - *Two edged sword of the spirit*
- The Holy Spirit - *Paraclete, Counselor, Comforter, advocator, intercessor, mediator*
- Gift of Righteousness and Truth - *Banner, Solid front, boldness*
- Shield Of Faith - *fiery darts quencher and interceptor*
- Helmet Of Salvation - *Hope, Protection of your mind and intellect*
- Ability to pray in the Spirit - *Confusion for the Enemy*
- Ability to watch with all perseverance - *Insight and sensitivity*

All these became effective weapons against the enemy because of the efficacy of the death of Jesus on the cross of Calvary and his subsequent resurrection.

Ability of each individual interest to be able to fortify itself with these self defensive and offensive mechanisms ensures protection and victory and that is what this level of investment is all about. Popularly referred to as "armor of God", they are like putting on a protective covering. These investments are spiritual; such are reliable protections even in your down time.

To the devil, crucifying Jesus on the cross was a victory upon God because at that time, Jesus was God's primary interest. God invested His Son with the motive of gaining the whole world. So, through Jesus, God the father had great expectations of returns. Satan was unaware of this but thought if he could contain Jesus' life in hell then he would win again. But God being great in planning and strategy kept the implications of this a mystery for four thousand years before Jesus was manifested.

Ten

MISSION ACCOMPISHED

The blessings that God bestowed on humanity were later called POWERS by Satan. The devil told Jesus that all these power will I give thee, and the glory of them; for that is delivered unto me and to whomsoever I will I give it. How did this so called power get to his hand? Adam was the culprit here, he was the one that delivered it to him because he did not know the actual intrinsic value of those blessings. Satan recognized these blessings and coveted them and eventually stole them from Adam through deceit. Satan knew that with the same blessings of Adam, he can rule the world and actually become the prince of the World, a title that belonged to Adam and descendants. So, not only was the power stolen from Adam, his title was also stolen.

> God had given him all the resources of heaven, for it pleases God that all the fullness of heaven should dwell in Christ. Jesus therefore becomes the treasury for all the resources of heaven and earth.

It was like a package. When Jesus eventually took the power from the devil, he declared them as the signs that follow believers-(Mark 16

17), and later called them the **keys of hell and of death**-(Revelation 1:18); he was referring to the same power.

Actually if we want to know what Jesus took back from the devil, we need to know what the devil took from Adam. And to know what the devil took from Adam we need to know those blessings that God bestowed upon the spirit of man in the beginning.

In other words, Jesus being the one that finally actualized the potential that existed in that initial blessing **came to fulfill the will of God in man**. He came to show us how we can live and maximize the potentials that God has built into humanity.

The first major investment made by the Chief Executive Director of Creations Investment Corporation were the infrastructures, facilities and empowerment provided for the managers but these were transferred to the competitors when the company came under a new management. The new management was able to maximally utilize the power to their advantage and to oppress the managers. The managers were at the receiving end of the oppression and each time it happened, they called it an **attack.**

The second major investment was sending one of the directors out to become a cleaner in the company under siege in a bid to save it; meanwhile, he had to leave a highly paid job, position and status behind. It later turned out that even while being a cleaner, he had the disposition of a manager with reinforcement from the headquarters. He was able to turn the table around and dominated the scene. He became the head and ceased to be the tail. He overwhelmed the new management with his wisdom and skills. All his proposals and undertakings were projected from the headquarters and never did anything without communicating with them. So, Jesus complied with the laid down policies and procedures of the main company and got the results desired.

Jesus came to live the life that God intended that man should live and he enforced it whenever necessary. Jesus Christ was able to manifest dominion, fruitfulness and replenishment, which are attributes with which God blessed humanity in the first place.

God's blessings to humanity were to *be fruitful, multiply, and replenish the earth, and subdue it: and have dominion over the fowl of the air and over every living thing that moves upon the earth (Genesis 1:28).*

The life of Jesus manifested all of the above attributes. Because he was able to manifest these attributes, he reigned in the face of any antagonism both from Satan himself, his cohorts, and the Pharisees that Satan instigated against him.

Jesus did not keep us ignorant of all he took back from the devil because he declared them to us like a victorious warrior would declare the spoils of war. Jesus actually took them back through a real battle, the cross being the symbol.

Jesus declared the spoils of that battle with Satan as the signs that follow the new creature. In Mark 16: 15-18, *Jesus said to the disciples: Go into the entire world and preach the gospel to every creature. He that believeth and is baptized shall be saved; but he that believeth not shall be damned. And these signs shall follow them that believe: In my name, they shall cast out devils, they shall speak with new tongues, they shall take up serpents and if they drink any deadly thing, it shall not hurt them, they shall lay hands on the sick, and they shall recover.*

These two statements in Genesis 1:28 and Mark 16:15-18 were made at two different times in the history of man but they both convey the same messages. They were both prophesies that stress two important characteristics that God wanted man to manifest in order to achieve his purpose here on earth. These characteristics are fruitfulness and dominion.

FRUITFULNESS:

God said be fruitful, multiply and replenish the earth. God meant this in the physical sense because God, a spirit being was relating to the physical planet earth and all His creation at that time. God also gave them everything they needed to be productive, profitable and increase in number by procreation because God wanted man to make this earth complete again with the supply of fresh offspring, a new creature after their own kind.

Similarly, Jesus' commandment to believers to preach to others about the kingdom of God meant multiplication and fruitfulness; but this time in the spiritual sense and that the kingdom of God should be planted in the hearts of men. Here Jesus was talking about evangelism and witnessing which will in effect get the people to believe and be saved. The gospel of Christ is the power of God unto Salvation to everyone that believes. Salvation leads to new birth spiritually because Jesus had determined that it is only the things of the spirit that gives life but the physical profits nothing. Believing in this gospel and consequently getting saved is the same as getting born again in the spiritual sense and this is what Jesus described to us in John 3:3 when he said *"Except a man be born again, he cannot see the kingdom of God".* Later in John 3:6, he said *"That which is born of the flesh is flesh; and that which is born of the Spirit is spirit".* So, when we are saved, we are born of the Spirit of God and therefore we are no more of the nature of Adam which was according to the flesh. At this point our spirit being becomes alive to the things of God. Paul called this a new creature, and with the new creature, the old adamic nature is gone; and a new spirit has come as Paul said in 2 Corinthians 5:17, *"Therefore if any man be in Christ, he is a new creature: old things are passed away; behold all things are become new."*

Preaching to other people about the kingdom of God is a way of being fruitful and multiplying the efficacy of Christ's suffering on the cross of Calvary. When the kingdom of God is preached and the people believe and get saved, their salvation translates to the birth of a new creature that has the ability to defeat the devil and make the devil fall again and again just like Jesus did in his earth walk.

Fruitfulness is life flowing from the life source. Once you are connected to God who is the source then you can bear fruit. It is very difficult to bear fruit when you are not connected with the source.

"I am the vine, ye are the branches; He that abideth in me and I in him, the same brings forth fruit; for without me you can do nothing." – (John 15:5)

DOMINION:

In the same vein, the blessing of dominion is synonymous with the signs that Jesus mentioned would follow those who believe.

Adam could no longer subdue the earth after he had sold out to the devil; he could no longer exercise dominion over the works of God's hands because he was then under the dominion of Satan. Adam was incapacitated by the devil. He could not manifest what God intended for him. But God still needed humans to subdue the earth, and still have dominion. And this was the reason for the plan of redemption.

The manager had become a cleaner because he yielded to the deceit of the competitors and failed to comply with the rules given by the Chief Executive Director. He therefore had no more say in the running of the affair of Creation Investment Corporation.

After his encounter with the devil and overpowering him, Jesus declared that anyone who believes in him will have the dominion that was lost to the devil back. Dominion is authority or ownership.

A man that cast out the devils is exercising dominion; even the one that takes up serpent or lays hands on the sick and they recover.

Jesus said "These signs shall follow them that believe; they shall cast out devils, they shall speak with new tongues, they shall take up serpents; and if they drink any deadly thing, it shall not hurt them. They shall lay hands on the sick, and they shall recover."

These are synonymous to the **blessings of dominion** that God gave to man in the beginning. At the resurrection of Jesus, this dominion was packaged in a different way and given another name – "**THE NAME OF JESUS**". Using the name of Jesus is exercising dominion and this is the way to confirm that Jesus Christ had actually sought and saved that which was lost by Adam. Remember in John 14:13-14 when Jesus said "And whatsoever ye shall ask in my name, that will I do, that the Father may be glorified in the Son; if ye shall ask anything in my name, that will I do." That was a prophecy. The efficacy of the statement would come after Jesus resurrected from the dead. He said it because he knew that he was soon going to combat the entire satanic forces, defeat them, make an open show of them, stripping them of their authorities and taking back the dominion with the rest of the power that were stolen from Adam.

Peter and John started manifesting dominion shortly after the resurrection of Jesus. The name of Jesus was used by Peter and John (Acts 3:6) to heal the crippled beggar at the beautiful gate after the death and resurrection of Jesus.

Jesus came to restore to mankind what the devil had stolen. Jesus is the way that God used to restore man to His perfect will, and your acceptance of him guarantees eternal life, dominion and the Holy Spirit dwelling in you. This is the simplicity in Christ. The gospel of Jesus Christ is all about the kingdom of God. Kingdom in its literary meaning is a domain subject to the authority of a king. The kingdom of God aims to make you a king in your own domain and it expresses itself in righteousness, peace and joy in the Holy Spirit. Therefore, to be a king in your domain you must manifest righteousness, peace and joy. *That is why the scripture later says that they which receive abundance of grace and of the gift of righteousness shall reign (as kings) in the realm of life by Jesus Christ. (Romans 5:17)*

In order to cast out the devils, you must have dominion. Jesus and Paul had dominion and that was why they were able to cast out the devil. This dominion differentiated them from the seven sons of Sceva who tried to cast out the devil using the name of Jesus without having the kingdom of God in them. The devil ended up casting them out of their clothing instead. This seems so funny but it is due to lack of dominion. Dominion will make a believer stand bold and unaltered in the face of the rage of the enemy. This is the kingdom of God and this is dominion.

The believer now has the word of God that will make him able to stand and say "It is written" just like his senior brother Jesus boldly declared during the temptation in the wilderness.

The source of power of a person of dominion is his reliance on God. Trusting God that what He said He would do. Knowledge that God is not a liar is Key. The dominion person says *"If God has said it, then I believe it, it is settled in heaven, and it shall manifest on earth"*. The dominion person can lay his hands on the sick and they shall recover by saying a simple prayer in the name of Jesus. This is the heritage of the new creature. And of course they have an intimate language, strange to the kingdom of darkness, which they use to exalt and praise their Father who is in heaven and build up the Holy Spirit who now dwells in them. Dominion belongs to people who know their rights and privileges in Christ and the Holy Spirit sees them as vessels in which He can invest His wonderful gifts.

Adam was blessed with dominion but he did not exercise dominion because he had no knowledge of his identity with God, and he did not know that there was an enemy of God out there who desired to have exactly what he had. Remember, the devil can now possess people and not only serpents, so, the devil may come in form of a man, a woman, a friend, a brother or a sister. The most important thing is not to be oblivious of the devices of the enemy, and then STAND.

When we operate in dominion we are masters over the laws of nature, because we have obtained the gift of righteousness and abundance of grace, and we can reign as king in the realm of life. The Holy Spirit in us is dominion. The Name of Jesus given to us is Dominion. The kingdom of God in us is dominion.

Access to Power is Conditional

Salvation is a pre-requisite to the manifestation of these signs mentioned by Jesus. Without believing in Jesus, it is impossible to manifest the signs that follow those who believe. This takes us back to the fact that Jesus came to restore us to our original position with God but the condition is to "BELIEVE". This seems so simple but that is God's way, He has created all things for His pleasure.

The Scope of the Power

The treasures that were hidden by Satan originally belonged to Adam. They only included the things of this world. The power that the devil claimed to have was seized from Adam and it could only govern the things of this world. All these changed hands as a result of Satan deceiving Adam. But they later changed hands again as a result of Jesus defeating Satan. The treasures are now hidden in Christ. They are integral part of the fullness of God in Christ. The totality of the fullness in Christ is not limited to what was taken from Satan, But the Power that Jesus claimed that were given to him exceeded that. Jesus said in Matthew 28:18 that *"All power is given unto me in heaven and in Earth".* This means that in addition to the power that Jesus took back from Satan, God had given him all the powers and resources of heaven as well, for *it pleased God that all the fullness of heaven should dwell in Christ.* Jesus therefore became the treasury for all the resources of heaven and earth.

So Jesus not only has all power on earth but he has all the power in heaven also. Jesus did not enthrone himself or honor himself with all these things but it pleased God the Father to make him the treasury and holder of all the resources of heaven and earth. For it pleased the Father that in Him should all fullness dwell (Colossians 1:19) and he gave him a name above all names (Philippians 2:9). The Father told Jesus, "Sit on my right hand, until I make your enemies your footstool."

Another constituent of the fullness of Christ is the divine nature of God which consists of the treasures of wisdom and knowledge, the life of God (ZOE), eternal life and all that God is. Mercy, grace, loving-kindness, longsuffering, goodness, truth, forgiveness are part of what God is and He showed all these glory to Moses on demand.

The Power of Resurrection is also a part of what God is, and Jesus said "I am the resurrection and the life", and this was what Paul wanted when He said "That I may know him, and the power of his resurrection, and the fellowship of his sufferings, being made conformable unto his death". This power of resurrection is basically the Holy Spirit, the same power that raised Jesus from the dead.

Eleven

THE COST OF THE POWER

God was glad with the status of His plan so far. The transaction has been made. Jesus has paid for the sin of man with His blood. The redemption of man was sure, though, not yet complete. Jesus brought His blood into the Heavenly Holy of Holies and God accepted it and gladly received His son, Jesus the Christ and gave him a seat in heaven right beside Him, making

> The devil still desires to rule over man therefore he is still employing the weapon of ignorance to cover the fact that he has been defeated, and of the knowledge that the key of power has been taken away from him.

Jesus the mediator of the new covenant. At this time the power taken from the devil was still with Jesus. The power is so valuable because retrieving it back was the reason for the four thousand years of meticulous and secretive plan of redemption; so, it had to be guarded jealously and securely. This power was not going to be entrusted in the hands of any man lest he gives it up to the enemy again like Adam did, but will be hidden in the safest place in heaven, where there is the highest form of security, and that is the right hand of the Father and guess who is sitting there – Jesus Christ.

It costed God the Father and Jesus a period of four thousand years of meticulous planning and secrecy. Also it costed Jesus having to leave all his glory and go to the world to suffer and die in the hands of the same people he was trying to save. It costed God a painful period of separation with His son Jesus. Also it costed God His power and authority given to Adam being used by the enemy against Him and His creatures for that long period of time.

Now, God did not give the key to any man. God instead gave the key to the church. The key was actually hidden in Jesus but Jesus is the head of the church. God simply promoted Jesus to a place where no power of darkness can approach and hid the key in him.

No doubt, the key is secure in Jesus who has been glorified and exalted, and the devil has been put to shame and cannot approach the place where Jesus is sitting. Therefore Jesus in a sense became the bank or the storage of all the fullness of God, in heaven and on Earth. God preferred to keep all these things in him because Jesus knew the value of this key since he knew what he suffered for it in order to take it back from the devil. It costs him his life, besides they went through the painful four thousand years of planning together when the power was in the hands of the devil and the devil was ruling over the works of God with the power of God and they can do nothing about it.

Remember Jesus did not do this only for the Jews or Christians or a particular sect of people but he did this for humanity as a whole.

He came to the world to establish a Church, which is a people who would believe in his mission, and he was going to take care of them and prevent them from being oppressed of the devil. He called this church his wife and gave his life for it. The key that dwells in Him, he has given the exact duplicate to the church. But he has the master key. He said whatsoever we bind or loose on earth will be bound or loosed in heaven. He will use his master key on our behalf through intercession with the Father.

The devil still desires to rule over man therefore he is still employing the weapon of ignorance to cover the fact that he has been defeated, and of the knowledge that the key of power has been taken away from him. In fact he still desires this key back. What do you think the devil is trying to do walking about like a roaring lion seeking for whom he may devour? What is he trying to devour in a believer? He already has the unbeliever in his net so he does not even care about devouring anything from them, but the believer has access to the key that he so much desires. Many a time, Satan struggles for this key with believers and after using all the resources he has, if he finally gets the believer to sin against God, then he discovers that the believer only has an access to the key through his BELIEVE in Jesus but the master key is kept in Jesus, in a place he cannot access. Then he realizes that he has tried in vain on that believer. But meanwhile, the fruit bearing capabilities of the believer is already hindered because of that sin, so, that believer needs to rejuvenate his fellowship with God by heeding to 1 John 1:9 that reads *"If we confess our sins, he is faithful and just to forgive us our sins, and cleanse us from all unrighteousness".* When the believer repents, his fruit bearing capabilities are restored, his gift of righteousness is reinstated, then the devil discovers that he has wasted his time all these while struggling with that believer because God has made provision for man's failure. If the believer does not repent, then he falls into the bondage of Satan. The good thing is that Satan cannot take the key back from a believer because the key is not with him or her. The key resides in Christ but we only have an access to use the key as if it is physically in our hands as long as we believe in the event of the cross. In case the devil really wants the key back, he cannot get it directly from us but needs to stage a fight with Christ himself who in turn is in God. But unfortunately, Satan can no more approach the place where Jesus sits talk less of fighting with him to get the key back.

Satan was eternally banished from God's presence

The devil used to be able to enter the presence of God before in order to accuse humanity in front of the Father but since Jesus took back the key from him; he lost his access to the presence of God. Jesus said *"I beheld Satan as lightening fall from heaven".* This statement made by Jesus was in two parts. An event that already took place in the past and a prophecy of an event that would take place in future. This was after the return of the seventy that were sent out to evangelize and they reported to Jesus that they had dominion through the name of Jesus (Luke 10:18, 19). It was not a coincidence that this event was linked to the expulsion of Satan from heaven because the power that allowed Satan's access to the presence of God was the power he seized from Adam and would soon be taken back. That power was in display when he appeared before God just before the tragedy of Job. That power allowed Satan all the privileges that God gave to Adam which included appearing in God's presence. When that power was taken back from Satan, he lost his ability to appear in the presence of God. This then became the second time that Satan would be expelled from heaven. The first time was before the creation of man. This was written in the scripture that we might know that Satan lost all the privileges he had as a result of the power that was stolen from Adam when Jesus took back the power. Satan no more has the power to accuse us before God. There is therefore no condemnation for us. This is one of the expected results of the plan that was kept a secret for four thousand years.

Twelve

JESUS' DEPARTURE WAS EXPEDIENT

Nevertheless I tell you the truth; it is expedient for you that I go away: for if I go not away, the Comforter will not come unto you; but if I depart, I will send him unto you. – John 16:7

Expedient in this context means advantageous, beneficial, worthwhile, wise or tactical. Jesus had the interest of the believers

Jesus knew that humanity lost the ability to perceive the things of the spirit using their spirit man hence they resulted in using their senses. In this state, human beings cannot know the Holy Spirit because He is a spiritual being and to know him, you must be walking in the spirit.

at heart and if he had continued here on earth, the benefits of resurrection would not have come to us. He knew that his departure to the Father would be beneficial to believers and the entire human race altogether. The only possible way for his departure was through crucifixion according to the grand plan. Crucifixion therefore became expedient, apart from being essential, critical and strategic. It was after crucifixion, resurrection and subsequent ascension that the Holy Spirit came.

Therefore the departure of Jesus instigated the next level of investment with God the Father, by investing another person of the deity in the person of the Holy Spirit.

Jesus knew that humanity needed the Holy Spirit in order to sustain the victory he has wrought because he has seen the ways of humans and understood it. He was sometimes astounded about the insensitivities, dullness and the inabilities of human beings to comprehend spiritual matters. After his resurrection and ascension, Jesus himself had to appear to two of the disciples on their way to Emmaus; when Jesus perceived that they did not have an understanding of what happened at crucifixion, He said ***"O fools, and slow of heart to believe all that the prophet have spoken: Ought not Christ to have suffered these things, and to enter into his glory?.*** Luke 24:25.

It is true that what actually happened at crucifixion was deep and concealed but Jesus had told his disciples both directly and in parables what was going to happen. At a time, he said it is expedient that I should leave you and only then will another comforter be sent.

Has it ever bothered you why the disciples of Jesus never knew him? Why they did not know what Jesus was all about and his purpose in life? Why were the disciples in darkness with the rest of the world about why Jesus had to go to the cross? Reading through the scriptures it seems that the disciples did not know anything **beyond what they saw,** even Jesus had to interpret his parables to them. Peter was about to break through the walls of spiritual realm when he walked on water with Jesus for a while but was again limited when he doubted and started to sink.

Why did the disciple not get it despite all the teachings, parables, transfiguration experience, direct speeches made by Jesus to inform them of the impending events? Many times, Jesus told them the details of how he was going to suffer and ascend to heaven but amazingly they still could not understand.

One would wonder why human beings relate perfectly to the physical things while we cannot even understand the things of the spirit of God despite the fact that the spiritual things are the actual things. The physical realm was called from the spiritual realm by the faith of God when He said "Let there be light". The word "Let" is a creative word. It requests, commands, warns and suggests.

Moreover, Jesus understood the position of man when it comes to the things of the Spirit of God. He knew our limitations. He knew why we are limited and how these limitations can be removed.

These limitations were introduced to humanity since Adam and Eve disobeyed God in the Garden of Eden. Their disobedience deactivated the spirit man, activated the flesh and limited them from understanding the things of the spirit. Instead of using their spirit man to comprehend the things of God, they started using their brains and other sense organs. They became limited to their five senses. God did not intend it to be so.

There was an account in Mark 8:17, where Jesus said *"Why reason ye, because ye have no bread? Perceive ye not yet, neither understand? Have ye your heart yet hardened? Having eyes, see ye not? And having ears, hear ye not? And do ye not remember? When I brake the five loaves among five thousand, how many baskets full of fragments took ye up?* They said unto him Twelve. *And when the seven among four thousand, how many baskets full of fragments took ye up?* And they said, Seven. And he said *how is it that you do not understand?* Can you imagine how Jesus felt about human beings? He seemed to be discovering a new aspect of human beings that astonished him. However, it is the inability to perceive things spiritually and that was why he made the statement below when he was about to die -

"Even the Spirit of truth whom the world cannot receive, because it sees him not, neither knows him: but ye know him; for he dwells with you, and shall be in you." - John 14:17

Here we see Jesus pointing out the attribute of a human being operating in the sense realm who cannot receive the Spirit of truth because He is not a physical being, and therefore they cannot comprehend and know Him. The Holy Spirit is a personality like Jesus, only a physical body was not made for Him like Jesus, so, he remains a spiritual being.

Jesus knew that humanity lost the ability to perceive the things of the spirit using their spirit man hence they resulted to using their senses. In this state, human beings cannot know the Holy Spirit because He is a spiritual being and to know him, you must be walking in the spirit.

This will change by the time they believe the work that Jesus had done, and the Holy Spirit will then dwell in them. Jesus knew that the world will have problem believing in what they do not see. Only those who believe in Jesus can know the spirit of truth.

One of the reasons why Jesus died was to remove these limitations. He knew that the Holy Spirit is the only one that can break the veil that limits human beings from the things of the Spirit and it is so important to Jesus that this limitation be broken so that humanity would be able to sense the things of the spirit through their spiritual antennae again.

At this time the work of redemption of man was not yet accomplished. Jesus was not yet seated at the right hand of the Father. Dominion had not yet been restored to man. Man was still under the dominance of the evil one. Even the disciples were still natural men, their spirits were not yet recreated and they lacked wisdom. Their spirits did not have the wisdom to grasp the riches of the work that God was doing for us in Christ Jesus, it can only be revealed by the spirit through revelation knowledge. This revelation knowledge later came through Paul the Apostle who was not even with Jesus in his earth walk. He said -*"But the natural man receives not the things of the Spirit of God: for they are foolishness unto him: neither can he know them because they are spiritually discerned."*(1 Corinthians 2:14). And he prayed –*"That the God of our Lord Jesus Christ, the Father of glory, may give unto you the spirit of wisdom and revelation in the knowledge of him: The eyes of your understanding being enlightened; that you may know what is the hope of his calling, and what the riches of the glory of his inheritance in the saints"* (Ephesians 1:17, 18)

In actual fact, it was expedient for Jesus to depart. The departure of Jesus brought a lot of blessings to us. It brought us the Holy Spirit, redemption, salvation, dominion, eternal life, abundance of grace, gift of righteousness, sanctification, wisdom. The language of the bible changed after Jesus died and resurrected. We started hearing words like Salvation, abundance of grace, eternal life, new man, new creation, inner man, gift of righteousness and many more. All these things were not available without Jesus dying for us on the cross. Jesus could not give them to us when he was here on earth, He needed to start his intercessory prayers with the Father before the Holy Spirit can be released to us.

At this time Jesus would become immortal as he used to be, timeless and endless. He Himself would no more be limited by the things of this world.

Thirteen

HOLY SPIRIT – THE LIMIT BREAKER

A mystery is anything that remains unexplained except by divine revelation. The explanation is only known to the insiders. The outsiders remain stunned with amazement and curiosity because they have not yet been clued in on that subject.

> The veil is not taken away until the hearts turn to the Lord. Only the word of God can make the heart of man turn to the Lord. The heart in this context refers to the Spirit of man.

Jesus explaining the meaning of his parables to his disciples said *"Unto you it is given to know the mysteries of the kingdom of God: but to others in parables; that seeing they might not see, and hearing they might not understand"*.

The scripture that says *"And the light shines in darkness; and the darkness cannot comprehend"*, perfectly fits the meaning of a mystery that is explained above. This is why born again Christians can understand certain spiritual details but the unbeliever would think it is foolishness. The life of God and the light of men are puzzling to the natural man. The senses cannot understand the faith in God because faith springs from the recreated human spirit. The darkness wants to talk about evolution and the big bang theory rather than creation and recreation.

The reason for this is that the Holy Spirit is needed to break the limitation to our comprehension of the things of the Spirit, and the Holy Spirit only comes into you when you have accepted the lordship of Jesus Christ. This is when the spirit of man is connected back to the Holy Spirit of God.

Jesus said, ***behold, I stand at the door, and knock: if any man hear my voice, and open the door, I will come in to him, and will sup with him, and he with me.*** *(*Revelation 3:20*)*. And later in Revelation 21:3, a great voice came out of heaven and said, ***"Behold, the tabernacle of God is with men, and he will dwell with them, and they shall be his people, and God himself shall be with them, and be their God.***

This is the means by which God planned to connect humanity back to eternity. The spirit of man connects with the Holy Spirit of God, and we become eternal beings again, and all things become new. There would still be physical deaths but the power of sin which is the strength of death had been broken.

This is a wonderful synchronization between the Director of Humanity Affairs and Director of Special duties in the persons of Jesus and Holy Spirit respectively. The only condition by which the Holy Spirit can indwell humanity is if they accept the lordship of Jesus Christ.

In John 4:10, Jesus talking to the Samaritan woman, challenged her to recognize the gift of God, and exchange the ordinary water with the living water. He went further to say in John 4: 13 that ***"Whosoever drinks of this water (ordinary) shall thirst again but whosoever drinks of the water (eternal) that I shall give him shall never thirst; but the water that I shall give him shall be in him a well of water springing up into everlasting life".*** In other words Jesus was telling them that the things which are seen are temporary and can depreciate in value; but the things which are not seen are eternal and can last forever.

Jesus also called himself the bread of life. He said the bread that the world knows profits them nothing. *"Your fathers did eat manna in the wilderness, and are dead"* (John 6:49). He then went on to say the most wonderful statement in John 4:51 that *"I am the living bread which came from heaven: If any man eats of this bread, he shall live for ever: and the bread that I will give is my flesh, which I will give for the life of the world"*.

When he figured that his disciples struggled to understand this, he pushed it further to say *"Except you eat the flesh of the son of man, and drink his blood, you have no life in you. Whoso eats my flesh, and drinks my blood, hath eternal life; and I will raise him up at the last day."* At this stage even his disciples murmured and they said this is a hard saying, who can hear it?

As this conversation progressed, Jesus unleashed the meaning of it all to them by saying in John 6:63 that *"It is the spirit that quickens; the flesh profits nothing: the words that I speak unto you, they are spirit, and they are life."* Even at this, many of his disciples went back and decided never to walk with him because they cannot just understand.

Jesus made another declaration in John 14:6 that *"I am the way, the truth, and the life: no man comes unto the Father, but by me"* and also in John 10:10 that *"The thief cometh not, but for to steal, and to kill, and to destroy: I am come that they might have life, and that they might have it more abundantly.*

It is amazing that Jesus had to go through all these trouble in order to make the people understand the truth, and even with all these explanations the people still did not understand.

Jesus was telling them the realities in him, his purpose in life, his future and the world cannot relate to it. He was giving them a full assurance of God's determination and commitment of providing eternal life for humanity and connecting them back to eternity. He knew that obtaining this eternal life is a major prerequisite for breaking the limitation of man from understanding spiritual things. Humanity missed it the first time when Adam and Eve failed to eat the Tree Of Life in the Garden of Eden. Now is their second chance; that same eternal life is in Jesus.

1 John 5:11 says **"And this is the record that God has given us eternal life, and this life is in His Son."** Humanity now has another opportunity to obtain eternal life by eating Jesus Christ, the bread of life. Jesus Christ has now been made available for us. Eating the bread of life in the person of Jesus Christ releases eternal life into us. If anyone accepts this Jesus Christ, such person will have access to the tree of life. The Cherubim with a flaming sword that was placed at the east of the Garden of Eden to deny access to the tree of life will be relieved his duty for your sake (Genesis 3:24). And you would eat and have eternal life. The limitations from the things of the spirit would be removed.

"For my flesh is meat indeed, and my blood is drink indeed. He that eats my flesh, and drinks my blood dwells in me, and I in him. As the living Father hath sent me, and I live by the Father: so he that eats me, even he shall live by me" (John 6:55, 56). Humanity has to live by Jesus in order to have the Holy Spirit dwelling in them. Jesus gave his total commitment and assurance to mankind on the condition that they eat his flesh and drink his blood. He likened it to the relationship between him and the Father and we know that Jesus was eventually raised from the dead by the power of resurrection sent by the Father because Jesus lived by the Father. In the same way, Jesus is promising the believers that he would raise us up in the last day, only if we eat him and live by him.

When Jesus said "**eat me**" he meant "**keep my commandments**", or "**believe in me**". He says "*If you love me, keep my commandments, then I will pray the Father, and he shall give you another comforter, that he may abide with you for ever.*"

The way Jesus lived by the Father was by "eating Him" that is "keeping His commandments" and "believing and trusting Him". Keeping Jesus' commandments provides a conducive environment for the spirit of God to be manifested in us. This is the promise.

The actual revelation finally came in 2 Corinthians 3:16, 17, 18 that *"Nevertheless when it (their hearts) shall turn to the Lord, the veil shall be taken away. Now the Lord is the Spirit: and where the Spirit of the Lord is there is liberty. But we all, with open face beholding as in a glass the glory of the Lord, are changed into the same image from glory to glory, even as by the Spirit of the Lord".*

That veil now refers to the flesh of Jesus which he demanded that we eat. By eating his flesh we have removed all hindrances that limit us from accessing the holy of holies. *"By a new and living way, which he hath consecrated for us, through the veil, that is to say, his flesh;"* – (Hebrews 10:20). It was God's doing when the veil of the temple was torn from top to bottom at Jesus' death on the cross to signify that the barrier between God and humanity has been removed and that humanity now has access to God due to the perfect sacrifice of Jesus.

Notice that the veil is not taken away until the hearts turn to the Lord. Only the word of God can make the heart of man turn to the Lord. The heart in this context refers to the Spirit of man. Before this time the Spirit of man was dead; in fact, every person born into this world was born with a spirit but this spirit is inactive towards the things of God. This spirit becomes active only by hearing the word of God. The spirit of man becoming active is the same as the heart turning to the Lord and it is the same as receiving eternal life; and only the word of God can make that happen.

The Spirit of God comes into the hearts of man only when it turns to the Lord and only at that time does the Holy Spirit administer the Kingdom of God through his workings and giftings.

This is when the Holy Spirit breaks the limit of the human senses, and the eyes of understanding become enlightened. This opens your eyes to the riches of the glory of God in Christ Jesus. It also enhances the ability to discern spiritual things and approve things that are excellent. If one's eye of understanding is not enlightened, the person can neither see beyond his nose nor appreciate the beauty in the things of God and His Christ.

The Holy Spirit is likened to a farmer who secures a land first before he starts to cultivate on it. This is what you do in real life before you can plant or build on a piece of land. The land must first be purchased or acquired; and this was done on the cross of Calvary when Jesus purchased us through his blood; this land represents the spirit of man. Jesus is our obtainer, while the Holy Spirit sustains us..

"For you are bought with a price: therefore glorify God in your body, and in your spirit which are God's" – (1 Corinthians 6:20).

The land is not fully owned by the new owner (the Holy Spirit) until a certificate of occupancy is issued; and this is what was done when the heart turns to the Lord. This certificate of occupancy represents the **will of man** allowing the Holy Spirit to come in. The Holy Spirit will not violate the will of man. The heart of man must willingly turn to the Lord through the hearing of the word of God. The heart turning to the Lord is a prerequisite before the Holy Spirit can start planting his seed into our Spirit and this seed is the **divine nature of God**. This is when the spirit of man becomes active to the things of God. It is only at this time that the Holy Spirit can carry out the ground breaking exercises that will eventually break the limit of our perception.

As we continue to hear God's word and yield our lives to the Holy Spirit of God, He continues to reinforce His strength in us through His fruits, and as we get more rooted and grounded in Him, He starts investing His gifts in us, and this initiates our being used as an instrument to do His work on earth.

The Holy Ghost will continue this transformation in us until we are changed into the same image of the Lord. Our own efforts cannot do the transformation but it is the Holy Spirit that does it.

The scripture goes on to say in Jude 1:24 that *Now, unto Him that is able to keep you from falling and to present you faultless before the presence of his glory with exceeding joy.* Again this is the Holy Spirit being referred to here; he continuously transforms us until we are what he wants us to be and He does this with exceeding joy.

Fourteen

OWNING THE RESPONSIBILITIES

The sin that was put on Jesus on the cross has been nailed to the cross and forgiven. This does not mean that man will no more commit sin but the final sacrifice for sin had been made by Jesus. All we need to do even if we sin is to repent. If we confess our sins, He is faithful and just to forgive us our sins, and to cleanse us from all unrighteousness. Blessed is he whose transgression is forgiven whose sin is covered and blessed is the man unto whom the Lord imputes no iniquity and in whose spirit there is no guile.

> We must admit that we had the corruptible nature of Adam, before we can claim the incorruptible nature of Christ. And this is exactly what we do when we say the sinner's prayer.

Jesus has blotted out the handwriting of ordinances like curses of the law, rules, and regulations, and decrees that were against us and contrary to us, that made us unrighteous, and replaced them with the grace of God that works through the golden rule of love. Most of all, He showed us the way to repentance which is a perpetual victory over the devil.

Jesus came out of Hell as a victor and rendered the devil eternally powerless. He became free from sin and so did we. Now he lives in righteousness and this righteousness, he imputed it on us. ***"For by one man's offence death reigned by one, much more they which receive abundance of grace and of the gift of righteousness shall reign in life by one, Jesus Christ*** – (Romans 5:17)

..Christ being raised from the dead dies no more; death hath no more dominion over him. For in that he died, he died unto sin once: but in that he lives, he lives unto God. *(Romans 6:7-10)*

One important thing to note is that just like the actions of Adam were binding on all human races, so were the actions of Jesus binding on all human race.

In fact before you can claim the victory in Christ, you must admit that you also fell in Adam when he fell in the Garden of Eden; the acceptance of this is a surety that Jesus actually bore your sins on the cross, and you died with him and resurrected with him.

Moreover, you can claim that you were in Jesus when he defeated the devil and that you and Jesus defeated the devil in hell. In other words, we must admit the corruptible nature of Adam, before we can claim the incorruptible nature of Christ. And this is exactly what we do when we say the sinner's prayer. *"I know I am a sinner but now I come to God in repentance, and want Jesus to be the Lord of my life"*. Every born again Christian must have said this prayer at least once. The prayer makes you own the responsibility of your sin and allows you to believe that your sin had been dealt with through the sacrifice on the cross. This is the only way to salvation approved by God.

For if we have been planted together in the likeness of his death, we shall be also in the likeness of his resurrection: knowing this, that our old man is crucified with him, that the body of sin might be destroyed, that henceforth we should not serve sin. *(Romans 6: 5,6)*

God is teaching us responsibility and humility here. He wants us to own our faults and surrender to his means of taking care of them. He wants us to be responsible for our actions and believe that he has already fixed the sin problem. He brought it home in 1 John 1:8,9 that *"If we say we have no sin, we deceive ourselves, and the truth is not in us. If we confess our sins, he is faithful and just to forgive us our sins and cleanse us from all our unrighteousness"*. That means he will absolve us despite our iniquity when we truthfully admit that we did sin. In other words, God will give us the incorruptible nature of Christ in exchange for the corruptible nature of Adam when we admit that we sinned. At that instant we are entitled to the gift of righteousness and abundance of grace which allow us to come into His presence with boldness. This is how the grace of God works.

The book of Hebrews 10:22 says, *"Let us draw near with a true heart in full assurance of faith, having our hearts sprinkled from an evil conscience, and our bodies washed with pure water"*. He is encouraging us to come to His presence with boldness and confidence. The way you approach His presence says volumes about your knowledge of Him. It determines how far you can go with him and also determines if He is your Father and God or just your God. Even after they have been forgiven, people still carry guilt of what they had done and had been forgiven. The father does not want us to come to his presence with guilt feelings. He wants us to purge ourselves from all of these before we come to his presence. In actual fact, those guilt feelings mean that you still regard iniquity in your heart; and based on that, He will not hear you. Those guilt feelings defile us before Him and the scripture calls them evil conscience from which God wants our hearts purged.

Fifteen

THE ORIGINATOR OF ALL THINGS

For about three hours before writing this chapter, song in the box kept reverberating in my heart.

All of a sudden, it dawned on me the magnitude of the power of God and his exclusive attributes. I realized that His divine power neither has an upper limits nor lower limits but fills everything that exists. It has given us all things freely to enjoy and even everything that pertains to life and godliness. This is the fullness of God in an inexhaustible measure

> O Lord my God!
> when I in awesome wonder
> Consider all the worlds
> Thy hands have made,
> I see the stars, I hear the
> rolling thunder,
> Thy power throughout the
> universe displayed:
> Then sings my soul, my Savior
> God, to Thee:
> How great Thou art, how great
> Thou art! ------

which cannot be quantified. The divine nature is eternal life but it is expressed in love and its manifestation is in the lights.

"In him was LIFE and the life was the LIGHT of men, the light shines in darkness; and the darkness cannot comprehend it" - John 1:4,5

It all started as LIFE in God, but when God said "Let there be light", the LIFE in God became LIGHT on earth and the physical realm was born. The source of that light was God himself because He literally called the light out of the abundance of the lights that was in Him. This is why there is no darkness in heaven, and Sun and Moon or candles are not needed to lighten heaven because the glory of God is enough to lighten the whole place. (Revelation 21:23).

God is the source of all lights. He is the Father of all lights. Life is to the spiritual realm what light is to the physical realm. Therefore that glory of God that lightens the whole heaven is LIFE in the realm of God and LIGHT in our realm.

Revelation 22:5, *"And there shall be no night there; and they need no candle, neither light of the sun; for the Lord God gives them light: and they shall reign forever and ever"*.

In eternity, there is no past, there is no future because everything appears as present to God. That is why God can go back and forth in time and still remains the same.

He is first, and yet the last, declaring the end from the beginning, and from the ancient times, the things that are not yet done. He is a dynamic God. This is because he operates from eternity. He exists in a state of equilibrium, which is a state of rest or balance attained due to the finished work. He created both actions and reactions to be equal and opposite, resulting in equal action of opposing forces, which is the force holding all things together.

Eternity is not bound by the restriction of time. Timelessness is an attribute of eternity, and this makes God himself timeless. With God there is neither day nor night and there is no concept of time. The concept of time did not exist until creation. Time is limited to only the physical realm and was created as references to the things that are done there. Time started when God created day and night on the third day of creation. Day and night were specially created for mankind when God positioned the sun to govern the day and the moon to govern the night, as a means of keeping track of the time, seasons and events. The creation is the initial investment of God to the planet earth, made in order to jumpstart his projects here on earth, so it is established that God has a purpose for everything he created.

Later God said in Genesis 8:22, *"While the earth remains, seedtime and harvest, and cold and heat, and summer and winter, and day and night shall not cease"* This tells us that the existence of the planet earth is the condition that permits time, and when the earth ceases to exist time ceases. God is not committed to uphold the concept of day and night after this physical realm passes away because that takes us right back to eternity where timelessness prevails.

The fact that the things of the Spirit of God are invisible to our naked eyes does not mean they do not exist. They do exist and in fact they are more real than the things that we physically see.

"While we look not at the things which are seen, but at the things which are not seen: for the things which are seen are temporal, but the things which are not seen are eternal". (2 Corinthians 4:18).

The things we see are the products of the things we do not see, proving to us that the spiritual is more superior to the physical. Amidst so many things that we can see, the sun and the moon are significant, everyone on earth see them almost every day and we see how intense their lights are. But the fact is that the light that emanates from the glory of God is greater than that from the sun because God made the sun from the abundance of the light that is in Him. God set these great lights –the sun and the moon in the firmament of the heaven to give light upon the earth. These are physical lights that are visible to our eyes. There are other lights that are invisible to our eyes and yet they were made by God from the abundance of the lights within Him. These lights exist in frequencies beyond or below the range of human visibilities.

The electromagnetic spectrum is made up of ranges of light waves containing tiny particles that are ordered in bands to form a continuous sequence. These are mainly divided into visible and invisible lights. In these sequences we have Gamma rays, X-rays, Ultraviolet, Infrared, Ultrasound, Microwave, and Radio waves to mention a few. The visible lights are a very small part of the electromagnetic spectrum, and they consist of the colors we see in a rainbow. The visible region is just an integral part of the big picture of the electromagnetic spectrum and lights from the sun and moon are in this region. We can as well say that the lights from the sun and moon are just an integral part of the lights that are present in God and yet we cannot sometimes withstand the heat that radiates from the sun as it scorches our heads and quickly drains energy from us and sometimes we need a sun shield or umbrella. Now, imagine standing in the presence of God without any shield. We all need a shield, and Jesus has become our shield.

Eternity only exists in the spiritual realm. Entities in this realm are immortal and there are no deaths. The physical realm is more limited and less resourceful because it was born out of the Spiritual realm and has been invaded by the enemy of God, Satan, who instigated death in the physical realm and caused deaths to happen.

The spiritual realm is real but invisible to our eyes. The reason why they are invisible is that they are made up of entities that exist in frequencies beyond or below the range of human visibility, pigments of the retina of our eyes cannot respond to these kinds of lights. Things in the Spiritual realm are entirely hidden from man, they are secrets kept from us. Even-though human beings have found ways to harness some of these lights and use them in Microwaves, wireless networks, radio, and television. Sometimes God can open our eyes to catch a glimpse of eternity and reveal a little bit of these secrets to man like he did to Abraham, Daniel and John, also scientists like Isaac Newton, Thomas Edison, and Albert Einstein and many more. God can reveal a segment of what is there in eternity. Matters in eternity are concluded; even our destinies are concluded and hidden in eternity.

The secret things belong unto the Lord our God: but those things which are revealed belong unto us and to our children for ever, that we may do all the words of the law - *Deuteronomy 29:29.*

Moreover, 2 Corinthians 4:18 says *"While we look not at the things which are seen, but at the things which are not seen, for the things which are seen are temporal; but the things which are not seen are eternal".*

The Spiritual realm, being eternal, is the place of our destiny. All things started there, and will continue there after this physical realm passes away. It is the realm that contains the throne of God where Jesus seats at the right hand side of the Father.

This explains God's nature and His omnipresence. Look at the atmosphere around you, it is filled with the nature of God, our bodily limitations may not allow us to see or touch it but it is there in form of invisible light. In fact the bible says *He is the Father of lights in whom there is no variableness, neither shadow of turning*- James 1:17. His word is light. It is quick, sharp and powerful just like X-ray; it is capable of piercing even to the dividing asunder of soul and spirit, and of joints and marrow, and is a discerner of the thoughts and intents of the heart. Do you catch that? X-ray itself is a form of light, quick, sharp and powerful, used to take pictures of the internal parts of the human body. The word of God serves the same purpose; quick, sharp and powerful, used to discern the thoughts and intents of the spirit of man, and divides joints and marrows.

"For as the Father has life in Himself; so has he given to the son to have life in himself". "And this is the record that God hath given us eternal life, and this life is in his Son" - *(John 5:26).*

Jesus was life first before he became the light of the world. The life was translated to our realm and became the light that the lenses of our eyes can accommodate and our minds can understand. This happened and the bible says *"And the Word was made flesh, and dwelt among us, (and we beheld his glory, the glory as of the only begotten of the Father,) full of grace and truth"- (John 1:14).*

The light of men in the physical realm is the manifestation of the life of God in the realm of the Spirit. Light comes to man as a result of the life of God that is in Christ Jesus.

The spiritual realm is richer than the physical realm because the physical is born from the spiritual, and therefore the life of God is richer than the light of men. This is why we need to draw life from God who is the source of all things because God has chosen not to force His life upon us.

Eternity exists first before the physical and when the physical comes to an end, then eternity continues forever and ever, never, never ending.

Sixteen

THE EYE OF FAITH

"For we are saved by hope: but hope that is seen is not hope: for what a man seeth, why doth he yet hope for? But if we hope for that we see not, then do we with patience wait for it" - (Romans 8:24,25)

The physical human eyes are available to see things in the physical and they are incapable of seeing spiritual things. This is why it is possible to see things in the spirit with your

> Whatever the eye of faith can see in the spirit, you can possess and manifest in the physical.

physical eyes closed but the same things cannot be seen with your eyes opened. Since spiritual things can only be discerned in the spirit, spiritual eyes are needed in order to see them. It has been mentioned earlier that spiritual things are eternal things. In eternity, there is no past, there is no future because everything appears as present to God; and there is no time restriction. The eye of the spirit, also referred to as the eye of faith, avails believers to see glimpses of eternity; such are called revelations or visions.

The word of God is living and active and has the ability to create things in the spiritual realm instantly. These things that are created in the spirit realm are substances of things hoped for, the evidences of things not seen in the physical realm. When the word of God is declared with faith, it immediately accomplishes its purposes in the spirit; but the physical realm has to wait for time before the same can be physically manifested. *"For the vision is yet for an appointed time, but at the end it shall speak, and not lie; though it tarry, wait for it; because it will surely come, it will not tarry."* – (Habakkuk 2:3-4). The vision in this context is referring to something that has already been accomplished in the spirit; even to prove its authenticity, the vision was being written down, however, it has to wait for an appointed or set time to manifest in the physical. It is only the eye of faith that can see these accomplished things in the spirit and this can shorten the time of manifestation. Faith is initialized in us by the studying and hearing the Word of God. Faith grows as the word of God in us grows. When we study or hear the Word, it penetrates directly into the Spirit of man and faith comes and when this Word continues to grow then faith grows. As faith grows in us, the ability of God inside us grows and the eye of faith sees more clearly.

The senses cannot understand the faith in God because faith springs from the recreated human spirit and the darkness cannot comprehend this because it does not understand creation not to talk of recreation. Faith is the power that transforms spiritually accomplished or approved things into physically manifested things.

These spiritually accomplished things are real in the spirit realm, just like any real thing that you can touch in the physical, but faith is needed to translate these things into the physical realm. The word of God is creative; when spoken it creates things instantly in the spirit realm. These things may have to wait for time in order to manifest in the physical but if your eye of faith is sharpened, you can see them and be able to bring them into manifestation even before the appointed time. This is one of the ways that things get accelerated in the spirit realm. Moreover, whatever the eye of faith can see in the spirit, you can possess and manifest in the physical. Many answers to prayers are hanging in the spirit realm but they need the power to translate them into physically manifested things.

Not that the prayers were not answered, but your eyes of faith have not beheld the accomplished things that have been done by the creator of all things concerning that request in the spirit. If you can see it with your eyes of faith, that will make tremendous power available to translate them into physical manifestation.

In fact many prayers pertaining to healing have been answered two thousand years ago but yet to be claimed by the owners and yet people die every day through diseases just because they lack the power to bring forth their miracles from the realm of Life that are invisible to our eyes into the realm Light that are visible to our physical eyes.

Physically, we can relate to it if a bank approves our loan application or if a promotion request is granted by our boss. We know immediately that these things exist and we can go and get them and take charge but we cannot relate to those things God had approved, accomplished or prepared for us that exist there in the spiritual realm. The reason for this is that our physical eyes cannot see them, only the eye of faith can.

Faith is a living thing. Faith grows, Faith can see, Faith can touch, Faith can move and can have knowledge and wisdom. Faith is needed in order to receive all the other gifts of the Spirit. Each of these gifts has its own potential to access the realm of the Spirit and translate invisible things to visible things, but we need faith in order to walk in all of them.

Our relationship with the Holy Spirit is what sustains the eye of faith. The closer we are to the Holy Spirit the sharper the Eye of Faith. The Holy Spirit is a major investment by God the Father for humanity. Jesus is our obtainer and the Holy Spirit is our sustainer. This is God's own way to connect us permanently to eternity. It was a massive investment.

About the author

Akin Isaacs Lufadeju, graduated as a Scientist and later went on to Executive Information Systems. He became proficient as a programmer / analyst. He has worked in various fortune 500 companies including AT&T Corp. and Union Pacific Corp.; also with Gallup Organization and Concurrent Technologies all in the United States of America before he relocated to Britain to continue his career. He now works as a Manufacturing Data Analyst/Application Developer with a leading manufacturing company whose portfolio boasts an unrivalled array of great brands in the United kingdom. He is combining his wealth of knowledge both in Science and Information Systems to develop applications that can be used for Overall Equipment Effectiveness, Key Performance Indicators, Performance management, Personal developments, Emotional intelligence, Continuous Improvement, Analytical and Automated reporting and other project management tools.

He is a Minister of the Word of God, passionate about telling others about Christ, and writing inspirational tracts and books for the purpose of helping others to come closer to the knowledge of God and His Christ. He demonstrated his flair for writing early in life when he wrote inspiring essays and poems that qualified him to compete in the senior league.

Isaacs and his wife, Lola, are involved in organizing Marriage Seminars, Married and Engaged Couples Events, providing marriage enrichment materials to couples for the purpose of maximizing the good things that God has given them to enjoy in their marriages.

Isaacs and Lola have been married for twenty one years and they have three loving children 'Rotimi, 'Tunde and Majesty.

About Life Beyond The Cross

Present book portrays God as the Director of a company called Creation Investment Corporation and describes Him as the most successful business person that ever stepped on the planet Earth. It all started by a decision to establish another branch of his company in another location which happened to be the planet earth which at that time was inhabited by a competitor who used to work for Him but things turned sour between them when he plotted to take over the business. To start his new branch off, he started by giving commands to the darkness, waters and winds. These all obeyed him. He appointed managers and empowered them to manage the business while he continued to manage the headquarters. The well being of those managers later became his heartbeat after they were deceived to step out of His laid down policies which eventually caused an economic breakdown and eventually a buy-out for the new branch. This was a distraction for this entrepreneur because he had excellent plans for the branch.

This book is all about what He did to take his company back from the hands of the competitors and restore the dignity of those managers, detaching his company from all unproductive influences by building an impenetrable business system.

I pray that as you read this book your eyes of understanding are opened and you are able to comprehend all the precious truth that God has uncovered through this book.

Akin Isaacs Lufadeju